Indestructible Foundations

Peter J. Wilson

Guardian of Truth Foundation
C E I Bookstore
220 S. Marion, St. • Athens, AL 35611
1-855-49-BOOKS or 1-855-492-6657

© **Guardian of Truth Foundation 2013.** All rights reserved. No part of this book may be reproduced in any form without written permission from the publisher. Printed in the United States of America.

ISBN 10: 1-58427-406-9

ISBN 13: 978-1-58427-406-3

Guardian of Truth Foundation
C E I Bookstore
220 S. Marion, St. • Athens, AL 35611
1-855-492-6657

Table of Contents

Lesson 1: The Arrangement and Value of Home Bible Studies 5

Lesson 2: God Is 11

Lesson 3: The Bible: God's Word 25

Lesson 4: Jesus Christ: The Son of God 35

Lesson 5: Authority in Religion 45

Lesson 6: Why You Need Christ 53

Lesson 7: Why You Need Baptism 61

Lesson 8: Why You Need the Church 71

Bibliography 83

DEDICATION

To my loving wife, Irene, of whom the inspired writer must surely have been speaking when he wrote, "Her children rise up and call her blessed: Her husband also, and he praiseth her, saying, Many daughters have done worthily, but thou excellest them all" (Prov. 31:28-29).

Editor's Note

This book has been edited and reformatted, requiring some minor changes in the book, although I am not aware of anything that affected the sense of what brother Wilson was writing (at least that was the intention).

Mike Willis, Editor

Lesson 1

The Arrangement and Value of Home Bible Studies

I. The Meaning of "Home Bible Studies" (or as they are often called "Cottage Classes").

The idea of teaching the word of God to individuals or groups of individuals in private homes is not a new or novel idea. It is simply restoring a fundamental emphasis in New Testament evangelism. It recognizes an inherent responsibility conveyed in the Great Commission to "go ye into all the world and preach the gospel to the whole creation" (Mark 16:15). This responsibility is shared by every member of the Body of Christ and cannot be done by proxy, nor is it the exclusive obligation of those devoting their full time to preaching the gospel. The attitude of the early Christians to this responsibility can be seen in such statements as this: "And every day, in the temple, and at home, they ceased not to teach and to preach Jesus as the Christ" (Acts 5:42) or " ... and teaching you publicly, and from house to house" (Acts 20:20). Just such an arrangement as I am advocating in this chapter was followed in Acts 10. Peter, a gospel preacher, was called to the home of a man named Cornelius to teach the word of God. In v. 24 we read "and Cornelius was waiting for them, having called together his kinsmen and his near friends" and in v. 33 Cornelius declares, "... now therefore we are all here present in the sight of God, to hear all things that have been commanded thee of the Lord." In every congregation today there are gospel preachers and other qualified teachers with the knowledge and ability to teach the same truths taught by the Apostle Peter and there are also many babes in Christ and others who feel that they lack such teaching ability but who have "kinsmen and near friends" who they can invite into their homes to study these important truths. This is my conception of what is often referred to as "personal work" ... it is simply to get every person in the congregation working in the all important work of "seeking and saving the lost." This was Paul's conception of how the church would grow and build itself up in the Faith as expressed in Ephesians 4:16 – "... according to the working in due measure of each several part, maketh the increase of the body unto the building up of itself in love."

II. The Practical Need for such an Arrangement Today.

Besides the scriptural implications of the passages already cited, the practical value of such an arrangement ought to be obvious as we view the situation confronting the church today. Twenty years ago gospel meetings were well attended by non-members and large numbers of baptisms were the rule rather than the exception in such efforts. With the present day competition from television, movies, sport activities, etc., the percentage of people just dropping in to visit services and the percentage of non-members who attend gospel meetings have decreased considerably. From twenty years of personal experience and from talking to many gospel preachers and examining their reports, I am persuaded that the greatest opportunity to reach lost souls today is through an emphasis on personal contact, by getting into people's homes for regular Bible studies. The present approach of many congregations is just not getting the job done. I know of dozens of congregations with the usual program of classes and worship periods and two or three gospel meetings per year who, despite the diligent efforts of a faithful gospel preacher and a number of experienced and informed Christians, are only baptizing fifteen or less people per year (a good percentage of whom are the children of members who have reached an accountable age).

What enthusiasm I have for the home Bible study program does not in any way reflect a lack of appreciation for the power of pulpit preaching, whether in regular services or in special efforts such as gospel meetings. That God has ordained the public proclamation of His Word cannot be denied and 1900 years has not changed either the Law of God or the pressing need for faithful gospel preaching. Home Bible studies and the contacts they afford simply enhance the opportunities to preach publicly to more and more non-members. It is a proven fact that there are some people who can be reached by this method that could not be reached through regular services or gospel meetings. Then, too, there is a greater concentration of truth made available to the prospect. How many people who you are able to get out to a gospel meeting attend every service of that effort? Such would be an exception in most places and yet it is a general rule that those consenting to attend a home Bible study attend all of the classes. It is also out of the ordinary for visitors to regular services or gospel meetings to ask the questions that may be in their mind about religion, but in the informal atmosphere of a home study, where such questions are solicited and encouraged, most people will open up and freely express themselves.

There is a fundamental law of God that applies to this situation. It is expressed in 2 Corinthians 9:6 – "But this I say, He that soweth sparingly shall reap also sparingly; and he that soweth bountifully shall reap also bountifully." Granted that Paul is here discussing the subject of giving, the fact is that he bases his argument upon God's fundamental law of sowing and reaping. It is not only true that we reap WHAT we sow but it is also true that we reap IN PROPORTION to the amount of seed we sow. When a program of home Bible studies are added to the regular preaching and teaching services, it simply increases the amount of gospel seed being sown in that community and, God's law being true, it will result in an increased harvest of souls. There is a question raised in Haggai 2:19 that is pertinent to our study, "Is the seed yet in the barn?" We provide comfortable buildings, we provide good gospel seed and insist that it not be mixed with human doctrines, we feast upon his seed ourselves and offer it to those few interested outsiders who will come to where we are dispensing it, but the reason the harvest is limited and often sparse is that the seed is not being taken out into the field and sown. In Matthew 13, Jesus said: "Behold, the sower went forth to sow." Why? Because he knew that the field would not come to him and that if there was to be a harvest, the seed had to be taken out and sown where it was needed. Dealing with the same responsibility under a different figure, Jesus said that he would make His disciples "fishers of men." A man may have the best fishing equipment and the best bait and sit in his living room and never catch a fish. Why? Because he knows that to catch fish you must go where they are. Jesus said in Matthew 17:27, "go thou to the sea, and cast a hook, and take up the fish." He recognized that to catch fish, you must go where they are. Does it not make sense then to suggest that in this business of fishing for men we would have a greater catch if every member of the congregation had his hook and line in the water instead of having just the preacher, elders, and few select teachers doing the fishing and the rest just looking on?

III. The Results of Such a Program Are Gratifying.

Until you have personally been involved in an active home Bible study program you find it difficult to comprehend the glowing reports of such efforts. One congregation had been baptizing 9 or 10 per year but baptized 86 the year that they began an efficient home Bible study program. One teacher alone had 94 baptisms in a two year period. My first attempt at such work was a series of classes we had at Sunnyvale, CA, in 1955. Over a six week period we conducted 13 classes per week. There was an average of 20 non-members attending, of whom thirteen were baptized. Using the material contained in this book, we later conducted 15 classes per week with an average attendance of 150 (of whom 20 were non-members). From these classes and contacts made in them there were 20 baptisms in a three month period.

In the last 20 years the Jehovah Witness Organization has increased 700% through the use of home studies. This growth was realized in spite of a doctrine that is contrary to the Scriptures and obnoxious to right thinking people!

NOTES

From the reports of others I have surveyed and from personal experience, it is a safe estimate to suggest that you can baptize 70-80% of those who attend a series of classes. How many baptize that percentage of visitors to a gospel meeting or at regular preaching services? I have taught as high as 18 non-members in a single class and yet have preached in many gospel meetings where I would have been happy to have that many non-members at a single service.

IV. "How Do You Get Classes Set Up?"

Many have come to me and said that they agree that the program is both scriptural and practical but say that they just cannot seem to get any classes going. Perhaps some suggestions along that line will be in order.

There are two general approaches to this work, both of which are good, and a combination of which will give new life and growth to any congregation:

1. Individuals need to be constantly striving to arrange classes with friends, relatives, fellow workers, etc. Brethren need to become "class conscious" in the sense that, rather than try to answer a question about instrumental music or the one church or baptism with a few hurried words, it is much better to say, "Why don't we set up a class one night a week to study some of these questions?" Even a small percentage of the congregation working at trying to set up classes can keep a preacher and several other teachers busy every night in the week.

2. In addition to the above, I have found that a series of classes for the whole congregation (arranged and planned, just as a gospel meeting would be) at least once or twice a year is most conducive to making people see the value of such a program. There are many preachers who are capable and willing to teach home studies and who announce to the congregation periodically that "I am willing to teach any class you can arrange," who are seldom able to keep more than one class per week going. On the other hand, with a planned congregational effort there easily can be 6-15 classes conducted per week (depending on the size of the congregation). The arrangement is simple. Ask those families who would agree to having a six or seven week study in their home to let that fact be known. Select as many homes as are needed in strategic locations in the community. Assign every member of the church to one of the classes (preferably in his own neighborhood) with an average of 8-10 members per class. Encourage those members to work in advance to get friends and neighbors in that area enrolled in the class. Since this is in addition to your regular program of preaching and teaching, you can realistically expect about 50-70% participation of members. However, the edification of those members plus the contacts with non-members will make the effort well worth the time and energy expended. The best qualified teachers in the congregation should be used. If there is a shortage of good teachers, the preacher, elders, or other qualified teachers can teach several classes per week each since the various classes will be scheduled on every week night (with the exception of the night of your mid-week service). I have found it useful when training teachers who are new to this type of program to meet with them all on Monday nights and teach them the lesson that they will be teaching in classes on the remaining nights of that week.

V. Some Specific Suggestions That Might Be Helpful.

NOTES

1. Size of Class. Any number from 2-20 can be taught in such a class with about 10 being the most expedient number.
2. Time. We schedule the classes to run for one hour after which the class is dismissed. Those who must leave may do so but I have found that some of the best discussions take place after class and very often run for several hours.
3. Teaching Method. While others may use and fine effective various methods, I can only recommend conscientiously that which I have found most effective. A lecture type class of approximately 45 minutes followed by a question and answer period of about 15 minutes has proven expedient for me. I usually set up the large charts on a tri-pod where everyone in the room can see them and also supply small 8.5 by 11 inch copies of the chart to be studied to each class member for his own use in taking notes, jotting down questions, for a permanent record of the study. (Note: Large charts with tri-pod and extra copies of the small charts in this book are available from the author.)
4. Class Order. While this type of class is less formal than others, one should guard against confusion and disorder that would hamper the study of God's Word. If there are small children around, it is best to have one of the ladies or teen-age girls take them all into another room to have Bible stories read to them.
5. Records. I have found it advantageous to keep an attendance record of each class taught with the address of non-members noted on the back of the attendance sheet. This helps to evaluate the results of the class and gives information in contacting prospects.

VI. **Special Note: Complete bibliographical documentation on all the books cited by author and title in the lessons that follow will be found in the Bibliography at the close of this book.**

NOTES

God Is

Psalm 19:1; Romans 1:18-22

Fact 1 The Universe Exists	*Fact 2* The Universe Shows Signs of Design and Purpose	*Fact 3* Man Possesses a Unique Nature
Choices 1. Something Came From Nothing. 2. Something Always Existed (A) Mind? (B) Matter?	*Choices* 1. Blind Chance 2. Divine Planning	*Choices* 1. Evolution 2. Divine Creation

The Alternative Cannot Be Proved

Lesson 2

God Is

Introduction:

A. "Does God Exist?" is without a doubt the most momentous and significant question that can occupy the attention of mankind.
   1. If we deny His existence we involve ourselves in many insurmountable difficulties (as we shall see later in the lesson).
   2. To admit His existence is to acknowledge Him as the greatest of all realities:
      a. He is the source of our life: "in Him we live and move and have our being (Acts 17:28).
      b. He is the Father of our Spirits (Heb. 12:9; Isa. 64:8).
      c. He is the Fountainhead of all Truth (Rom. 11:33; Jas. 1:17).
B. Beyond any doubt then the knowledge of Him and His will is the greatest knowledge we can attain to, and is worthy of our time and most diligent efforts (John 17:3; Jer. 9:23).
C. Every Christian should strive for both the knowledge and courage to meet the skeptic and to "give a reason for the hope that is in you" (1 Pet. 3:15; Jude 3; Phil. 1:17)
D. The three most prominent positions regarding the proposition:
   1. Theism – Belief that there is one God, Creator of Heaven and Earth, Father of our Spirits, Source of Righteousness and Truth, and Object of Worship and Reverence.
   2. Atheism – Denies the existence of God and seeks to prove that He does not exist. (We will show later that it is absolutely impossible to sustain this position.)
   3. Agnosticism – Does not believe that the existence of God is capable of proof one way or the other and hence frankly admits "I do not know."
E. Limitations of our study.
   1. Remember that the being and will of God are matters of Divine Revelation ("the world by its wisdom knew not God," 1 Cor. 1:21).
   2. The Bible does not argue the existence of God; it is a fact recognized from the first verse on.
   3. To the person who rejects the Bible as a revelation from God, the best we can hope to do is to show that, based upon our observation of the universe about us and the nature of our being, it is more reasonable to believe in God than not to.
      a. That God recognized the validity of such evidence is seen in these passages (Psa. 19:1; Rom. 1:18-22).

I. The Universe Exists.

A. The fact is so self-evident that it needs no proof. To deny it would be to deny our own senses and consciousness.
   1. But something cannot come from nothing.
      a. Every effect must have a cause.
         (1) Every plant, tree, etc. came from a seed which in turn came from another seed, etc.
         (2) Every creature, man or animal, came from parent stock, who in turn came from their parents, etc.
         (3) Every effect we observe in the universe had a cause, something or someone who brought the effect about.
   2. Even the atheist does not deny this obvious fact. The question resolves itself into this proposition: Since the Universe exists, and something cannot come from nothing, then something (or someone) has always existed.

a. The atheist and the materialist say that it is matter that is eternal, that from some unexplained and supposed explosion of dead matter, the fragments that form this universe were formed and that by some unproven spontaneous generation and evolutionary development, plants, animals, and men came into being.
b. The Christian, on the other hand, affirms that Mind (God) has always existed and that He originated and was the designer and planner of the Universe (Psa. 90:2).
3. Why we believe that Mind (God) is eternal rather than the materialistic view.
    a. Mind is greater than matter.
        (1) Mind knows, matter is the object known.
        (2) Mind moves, directs, and modifies matter.
            (a) By Mind, lightning is chained.
            (b) By mind, the power of steam is controlled.
            (c) By mind, the strength of a lion is subdued.
        (3) Surely the tree is not greater than the craftsman who cuts it down and shapes it into a beautiful piece of furniture.
        (4) Surely the chemicals are not greater than the chemist who combines those chemicals into useful products for man's use.
        (5) If dead matter produced the universe and man, who has intelligence, then it produced something greater than itself.
    b. Matter is not intelligent.
        (1) The tree cannot turn itself into a polished piece of furniture.
        (2) Iron ore cannot turn itself into metal and the metal into a machine.
        (3) It takes mind (intelligence) to direct control, and shape the dead materials of the Universe. (For full discussion of this point see *The Divine Demonstration*, Everest, 124-130.)
    c. Matter is not eternal.
        (1) Not only does the Bible teach that the material creation had a beginning (Gen. 1:1) and will come to an end (2 Pet. 3:10), but science has now come to the same conclusion. Note the following from *Modern Science and the Christian Faith*, 11:

            "Science formerly taught the 'conservation of matter,' i.e. that matter was indestructible, that we could change its state but we could neither add to nor subtract from the total amount of matter. Today, science teaches that matter can be changed into radiant energy such as light or heat and cease to exist as matter. ... In this day of atomic bombs and atomic energy, it is not necessary to pile up evidence that matter can be changed to energy" (21). "These all indicate a beginning or a creation of the Universe. Every star is losing energy and mass. They must, therefore, have a beginning."
        (2) It is certainly more reasonable and logical, then, to accept the Biblical truth that "In the beginning God (Eternal Intelligence) created the heavens and the earth" than to accept the alternative that "In the beginning, matter (dead, senseless, passive) created the heavens and the earth."

II. The Universe Shows Signs of Design and Purpose.

    A. Consider the immensity of the Universe:

        1. "This earth upon which we live is a tremendously big something. But it is a mere speck when compared with the sun which is a million times bigger. The distance around the earth in round numbers is 25,000 miles. But the distance to the sun is 4,000 times as great as the distance around the earth, being about 92,000,000 miles. Neptune is said to be two and one-half billion miles away or thirty times as far away as the sun.

        "Sirius, the brightest star of the heavens is fifty-one million million miles away. The distance to many of the heavenly bodies is so great that it is measured in terms of 'light years.' Some of them are said to be thousands of light years from the earth. This means that thousands of light years are required for light, traveling at the rate of 186,000 thousand miles per second to reach us from these bodies" (Kelley, *Why I Believe in God*, 13).

        "We are told it takes light 100,000 years to travel from one edge of our galaxy to the other ... our galaxy has a hundred billion stars and there are beyond our own milky way galaxy at least a billion more galaxies, each one has approximately as many stars in it as our galaxy" (*Scientific American*, Sept., 1956).

        Our finite minds may find it difficult to comprehend the vastness and complexity of the Universe in which we live but no person could fail to see design and purpose in it all (Rev. 4:11).

    B. The design and purpose of the Universe itself.

        1. In spite of the innumerable stars, planets, and even galaxies like our own, in spite of differences in the size and speed of these heavenly bodies, they all operate with mathematical precision. They do not collide with and destroy one another, they do not operate by mere chance. There is such order and design in their movements that scientists can foretell an eclipse of the sun years in advance (to the minute) and can chart the position of planets for years to come.

        2. The Universe not only shows design but a purpose and plan to make life possible on the earth. "The rotation of the earth on its axis, for instance, is 1,000 miles per hour at the equator. If it were 100 instead, the days and nights would be ten times as long, the result of which would be the burning up of all vegetation each long day and the freezing of each surviving sprout each long night. The sun, the source of light, has surface temperatures of 12,000° Fahrenheit, the earth is far enough away for the right warmth, not too much, not too little. If the sun gave less radiation, the result would freeze us all, and if more it would roast us all. The slant of the earth is at an angle of 23°, which give seasons, and if not so tilted, the movement of the vapors of the sea would turn continents into ice. If the moon were set at less distance from the earth tides would submerge all continents twice daily, and the mountains would erode away. If the crust of the earth were ten feet thicker, there would be no oxygen and all life would die, and if the ocean were a few feet deeper, no life could exist. If the atmosphere were thinner to the point of precision, meteors which hurl from their orbits and dart toward the earth and which now burn and consume in the atmosphere, would shoot to ground and set fires over the whole earth, all of which is proof that life was created, is governed by mathematical laws and is not an

NOTES

accident" (F. E. Wallace, *Bulwarks of the Faith*, I I: 332, 333).
3. This design and purpose is seen not only in the overall scope of the Universe but is equally as marvelous even in the minuest detail.
   a. Men still marvel at the detail and plan of each individual snowflake.
   b. The smallest cell of a living organism is many times more complex than an IBM machine.
   c. Men have come to realize that each tiny atom has a well ordered universe of its own within it.
   "All that we see, trees, houses, people, etc., are composed of these tiny atoms ... and that gives us this phenomenon: an infinitestimal planetary system within an already infinitestimal planetary system! And it's all so small that the inner core occupies only a thousandth of a millionth of a millionth of the space within the atom" (*World Within the Atom*, Columbia University Press).

C. The Design and purpose of the human body.
   1. The Psalmist exclaimed, "I am fearfully and wonderfully made" (Psa. 139:14). The longer men study the human body, the more they realize that it is a masterpiece of intelligent and superhuman planning.
      a. We see a telescope that can bring distant objects into focus, it can be adjusted for objects near and far, can be placed on a tripod to swing easily from side to side, and has a lens that is curved so that the light will be refracted to give a distinct image. If we had never seen one before, we could, upon examination, come to no other conclusion than (1) it is the result of intelligent planning ... it did not just happen (some parts could not have accidentally fallen off an opticians bench and assembled themselves into that instrument), and (2) it is obviously designed for the purpose of observing objects.
      b. But then we examine the human eye and find an optical instrument far more intricate and functional than the finest telescope.
         (1) The different humours through which the rays of light pass correct what would otherwise be an imperfect impression due to the separation of some of the colors.
         (2) The eye is self-focusing and with the same lens can perceive objects in varying distances from a few inches to several miles instantaneously.
         (3) The eye has a self-adjusting shutter in the iris which expands or contracts yet always maintains a perfect circle, and the pupil contracts automatically if too much light is being let in! (Automatic shutters and self- focusing lenses are among the very latest discoveries in the complicated field of photography, yet such ingenious ideas were built into the human eye from the beginning.)
         (4) The eye can perceive objects in different directions, for it is hinged in such a way that it can turn with the greatest rapidity right or left, up or down, without even moving the head.
         (5) The eye has a self-cleaning mechanism. In telescopes and fine optical instruments, great care is taken to keep the lens away from dirt particles and they must be period-ically cleaned to be efficient. But the eye has his special fluid built in, keeping it both

moist and clean, while the superfluous liquid passes through a hole in the bone of the nose where it is evaporated.
- (6) Our admiration for this amazing mechanism is further enhanced when we realize that it was a "prospective" organ, formed before birth (and of no use at the time it was formed) to do a job later on.
- c. Now, who is willing to say that the telescope is the product of intelligent planning and purpose but that the eye, that excels it in many ways in intricacy and utility was just the product of chance?
  - (1) Whether we understand all there is to know about the eye or not is not the point. The fact is, just a superficial examination of it proves to our mind that it was designed by intelligent planning to serve a specific purpose.
- d. Of course, the argument is made even stronger when we consider the following:
  - (1) An eye is not found in one man alone but in millions of men, each showing the same marks of design.
  - (2) The eye is provided in duplicate in each person and so the two eyes are adjusted that they can work together or separately.
  - (3) The eye is only one of hundreds of organs and parts of the human body. Each part separately shows the same amazing design and planning, so much so that modern medicine has tended more and more to specialization (a man devoting the majority of his study and work to just one part of the body) because each part of the human body is an inexhaustible field of study and work.
- e. The identical argument on design and purpose can be made concerning every organ of the human body.
  - (1) Who will say that pumping systems that pump water through the various parts of a large city are the result of intelligent planning and engineering but the human heart, which pumps about 6,000 pounds of blood through the 10,000 arteries and veins of the body every 24 hours and can operate for 60 to 90 years without shutdown or repair (and which, in some instances, repairs itself) is the result of blind chance?
  - (2) Who will say that the telegraph and telephone systems of a city are the result of brilliant engineering and planning but that the human nervous system with its system of messages and impulses from the brain to every part of the body (and can again operate in most cases for 60 to 90 years without repair) is just the product of blind chance?
  - (3) Who will say that Univac and other "electronic brains" are examples of extraordinary planning and design but that the brain after which it is designed and the brain that conceived and put it together is just the product of blind chance? (For full discussion of this argument, see *Paley's Works*, II: 8-20 and *Truth of Christianity*, Turton, 16-20.)
D. The design and purpose of plant and insect life. (Morrison's book *Man Does Not Stand Alone* and Meldau's book *Why We Believe in Creation Not Evolution* contain a host of fascinating examples of the design and purpose, seen in these realms. We mention just a few to illustrate the principle. – P.J.W.)

NOTES

1. "The mosquito has a perfect tool kit. It is carried in the beak, which is a long slender sort of nose. The tools are sheathed in a well-fitting pocket of soft skin which is really the mosquito's lower lip. Inside the cover are six long neat tools, a pair of saws, a pair of lancets, a syringe, and a syphon" (Meldau, 102).
2. The water spider makes and uses a tiny diving bell. "The tiny, inverted nest of silk is anchored firmly under water ... a watertight air chamber. The spider then fills it with air by trapping a bubble between its hind legs: the air in this bubble is released into the nest. Fresh air is brought down to this diving bell as often as required until the family is raised" (ibid., 101).
3. Balloon spiders spin parachutes of silk which they use to transport themselves across fields or as far away as a hundred miles (102).
4. The tent caterpillar lays down guide lines as it travels from branch to branch on a tree and then follows those lines back to its nest in the evening (102).
5. The water scorpion has a "snorkle" type tube so that it can breathe fresh air while submerged (102).
6. Cacti and other succulent plants of arid regions store water during the rainy season to carry them through the many dry months (99).
7. Milkweeds, dandelions, etc., have a white sticky sap so that when ants and beetles seek to climb up the plants, their pick-like claws pierce the tender tissue, letting a tiny droplet of sticky milk gush out and the sticky liquid soon discourages the trespassers (100).

E. To summarize the argument then. The Universe in all of its aspects is a masterpiece of intelligent planning. All science is predicated upon the proposition that the visible Universe is intelligible. It is built on laws that can be ascertained, observed, and catalogued. The question then is "from what source can intelligibility come except from intelligence?"

To say that all of this is "Nature" does not answer the question, for if they mean by "Nature" some source of intelligent planning, they are simply using a different name for God. If they mean by "Nature," dead, senseless matter then they still have not accounted for the design and planning of the Universe.
1. Since the Universe is run by laws, there is a Lawgiver.
2. Since the Universe operates on mathematical principles, there is a Mathematician.
3. Since the Universe itself and the smallest atom in it are masterpieces of engineering skill there is an Engineer.
4. Paul in Hebrews 3:4 made the same argument when he said, "Every house is builded by someone (the house proves the builder – PJW); but he that built all things is God."

III. Man Possesses a Unique Nature.

A. That man is a unique part of the creation is undeniable. He possesses characteristics and faculties that are not only unknown to the highest form of animal life but which, from the very nature of the case, could not have been the result of a gradual development from the animal kingdom.
B. Again, we are faced with two choices as to how we shall account for man's existence and nature:
1. Man was created by God (Gen. 1:1, 11, 21, 25-28; 2:7).

        a. This accounts for his origin.
        b. This accounts for his intellect, his religious intuition, his aesthetic appreciation, his moral consciousness.
        c. This accounts for his dominion over the animal world (Psa. 8:4-8).
    2. Man is the product of evolution.
        a. The difficulties of this position we will explore in a moment but for the time being a passage from Isaiah 29:15, 16 is well to keep in mind. "Ye turn things upside down! Shall the potter be esteemed as clay; that the thing made should say of him that made it, He made me not, or the thing formed say of him that formed it, He hath no understanding (intelligence, American Translation)."
    3. The supposed third choice, "theistic evolution," is really no choice at all.
        a. Evolution, as defined by Earnest Haekel, is "the non-miraculous origin of the Universe," hence God is ruled out.
        b. "Theistic evolution then is a contradiction in terms. To maintain that evolution can be theistic is as inconsistent as to claim that falsehood can be true" (Higley, *Science and Truth*, 31).
        c. The same class of men who refuse a literal application of Genesis 1 and 2 are the same ones who deny the "literal" virgin birth, the "literal" resurrection, the "literal" miracles, and the "literal" atonement; and who "spiritualize" and "symbolize" the Lord right out of business making the Christian religion a farce.
C. Why we reject Evolution as the answer to man's existence and nature.
    1. It is an unproved theory.
        a. There is a difference between science (a body of absolute knowledge) and the theories of men in the field of science.
        b. "Theory" is defined as "a belief not yet tested in practice" or "a hypothesis," or "something assumed as a starting point for scientific investigation."
        c. If evolution were always identified for what it is, an unproved theory (or rather, 17 different and opposing theories), instead of being taught as a proven fact of science, the faith of many unsuspecting young people would not be shaken by their contact with it.
        d. Quotations from prominent scientists putting evolution in its proper perspective:
            (1) Sir Arthur Keith (British Museum): "Evolution is unproved and unprovable."
            (2) Two professors from Aberdeen and Edinburgh in the book, *Ideals of Science and Truth*: "We do not know whence man emerged, nor do we know how man arose, for it must be admitted that the factors of the evolution of man partake largely of maybe's which have no permanent position in science."
            (3) Prof. Fleischmann, Zoologist of Erlangen: "The Darwinian theory of descent has not a single fact to confirm it in the realm of nature. It is not the result of scientific research, but purely the product of imagination."
            (4) Sir William Dawson, Canada's great Geologist, said of evolution, "It is the strangest phenomena of humanity; it is utterly destitute of proof."

NOTES

(5) Dr. Robert Millican, Physicist and Nobel Prize winner: "The pathetic thing is that we have scientists, who are trying to prove evolution which no scientist can ever prove."
2. It does not account for the origin of man.
   a. If all of the accounts of development within various species are granted, that still does not explain the origin of life.
      (1) Life comes from life ... this is a scientific fact! There is life in a million different forms all about us. Where did it come from? If not from a creative God then dead matter produced it. This can never be proved.
         (a) Charles Darwin: "The mystery of life remains as impenetrable as ever."
         (b) Sir Oliver Lodge: "All the many attempts in the direction of spontaneous generation have failed."
         (c) Dr. John Coulter: "The study of evolution has nothing to say concerning origins. When one goes beyond the observed changes and tries to trace the successions back to their source, he is in the region of speculation and outside the boundaries of science."
3. Not only does it have no proof for the beginning of life but two-thirds of the whole chain is missing!
   a. Anthony Standen, Scientist, in the book, *Science Is a Sacred Cow*, says of the phrase "missing link": "It is a most misleading phrase, because it suggests that only one link is missing. It would be more accurate to say that the greater part of the entire chain is missing, so much that it is not entirely certain whether there is a chain at all" (106).
   b. "The first assemblage of organisms is found in the Cambrian rocks" (*Man and Biological World*, 352).
      (1) They tell us that there has been life on the earth for two billion or even three billion years, yet admit that the earliest fossil record is only one-half billion years old. Hence, by their own admission, at least 2/3 of the whole theoretical chain (that is supposed to trace man back through a graduated series of animals to the tiniest one-celled animal) is devoid of proof!
   c. The real issue with Evolutionists is not whether there has been development and improvement within a species but whether there has been "transmutation," the crossing of the line between vegetable and animal and animal and man.
   d. But, many ask, "What about all of the pre-historic men we have seen pictures of in textbooks?"
      (1) Many assume that these furnish the link between man and ape.
      (2) Many also assume that whole skeletons have been found to bridge this gap. But such is not the case!
         (a) The Heidelberg man, discovered at Heidelberg, Germany, in 1907 consisted of one jaw.
         (b) The Java man was put together from a cranial cap, a thigh bone, and a few teeth. It could not even be proved that they were from the same creature.
         (c) The original Peking man consisted of one tooth!

NOTES

(d) The Piltdown man that was considered *by Encyclopedia Brittannica* to be the greatest find of the century and is still to be found in some textbooks was proven to be a hoax in 1954. (If most of the greatest scientists in the world were taken in by this fraud, how can we trust their scholarship on the others?)

(e) Dr. Austin Clark, Biologist of the Smithsonian Institute said, "Man is not an ape and in spite of the similarity between them there is not the slightest evidence that man is descended from an ape … there are no such things as missing links. Missing links are misinterpretations."

(f) Dr. E. A. Hooten: "These alleged restorations of ancient types of man have very little if any scientific value and are likely to mislead the public … so put not your trust in reconstructions."

4. It fails to account for the characteristics man possesses which are completely unknown to animals.

   a. Man has the capacity for rational thought.
      (1) This is to be distinguished from the teaching by "instinct" that is used in training a bear to skate, a horse to count, etc. An animal does not have the intellect to train other animals, to accumulate knowledge from generation to generation, to build machines and tools to lessen his work, etc.
   b. Man has a sense of morals.

   "Man alone of all earthly creatures does wrong. Willfully or ignorantly he disobeys the laws of his nature or fails at complete fulfilment even when desiring it. Theft is no crime in a monkey or a bear. Bloodthirstiness is no vice in a tiger, nor vanity in a peacock. A dishonest or cruel or vain man breaks the laws of his own nature" (Hamilton, *Basis of Faith*, 221).

   Have you ever seen anything that shocked your sense of moral decency? If so, at that moment you exercised a faculty possessed by man that is unknown to animals.

   c. Man has an aesthetic nature. Inherent in man is the capacity to appreciate and enjoy the beautiful and harmonious. A monkey or dog or cow are unmoved by a beautiful painting, an exquisite orchid, a beautiful sunset, etc.
   d. Man is inherently religious. Even the most primitive civilizations have had a sense of a higher being, a basic fear of death, a conception of a life after death, and a form of worship. Evolution has failed to account for the fact that animals are completely devoid of this inherent religious intuition.
   e. Man has a conscience. While not an organic part of his body, nor anything that he could have inherited from supposed animal ancestors, it is a real part of our being.
   f. All of these marks of personality in man prove two things:
      (1) He was created in the image of a "personal" God with those same qualities of intellect, free will, moral sense, etc., and was not the product of so-called "resident forces" in the material Universe.
      (2) There is something in man that is not material. Scientists tell us that our bodies are constantly changing … that our bodies today (including our brains) do not contain

NOTES

a single atom or molecule which they contained ten years ago. Yet our personality, our memory of who and what we are, our moral consciousness, and intellect are still present. We must have something else besides atoms and molecules.
5. All of its vaunted "proofs" have fallen by the wayside of true scientific progress.
   a. Lamark's theory of "acquired characteristics" that was so widely acclaimed earlier has been discarded. *Life Magazine* (March 17, 1947), says, "Until 1900 many biologists believed that the characteristics plants and animals acquired from their environment were passed to their offspring. Modern genetics has proved they are not."
   b. Darwin's theory of natural selection has been rejected. In his book, *The Meaning of Evolution* (230), George Simpson, Curator of the American Museum of Natural History, announced that Darwin's theory of natural selection was "bound to be wrong."
   c. Mutations produced by radiation were supposed to be the answer for evolutionists but here again, in spite of all the experiments which have produced an amazing number of varieties, 99% of which have been harmful), there has still been no evidence whatsoever of transmutation (the crossing of species). Experiments by Prof. H. J. Muller of the University of Indiana on a little fruit fly, have, by radiation, produced the equivalent of 1/2 million years of human evolution. But did it turn into a bumble bee or a June bug? No, they changed its eyes from red to white and back again, its wings from long to short and back again, but it is still nothing but a fruit fly.
   d. Vestigial organs were once considered strong proof by evolutionists. These so-called "leftover" organs were supposed to be carryovers from previous life forms no longer useful in our present development. In man, they used to list 180 organs including such things as the thyroid gland, pituitary gland, etc. Of course, modern medicine has shown the uses of all but a few of these 180 organs and Prof. E. S. Goodrich of Oxford University says, "He would be a rash man indeed who would now assert that any part of the human body is useless."

   Along this line, one of the strongest arguments against evolution is the absence of "Nascent organs" or organs in the process of developing for use in the next stage of development. "Although the anatomy of thousands of species of animals has been carefully studied, it is impossible to name a structure in any of them which is even probably in a nascent condition" (De War, *Transformist Illusion*, 166). In other words, no fish has half formed legs in preparation for the transition to amphibian, no reptile has half formed wings in preparation for the transition to bird life, no species of ape has a half formed soul (conscience, moral sense, capacity to worship, etc.) in preparation for becoming a man.
6. Its logical consequence is the selective breeding of human beings.
   a. Darwin's *Descent of Man* (1874 Edition, 149-150), "With savages, the weak in body or mind are soon eliminated; and those that survive commonly exhibit a vigorous state of health. We civilized men, on the other hand, do our utmost to check the progress of elimination. We build asylums for the imbecile, the maimed, and the sick; we institute poor laws; our medical experts exert their utmost skill to save the lives of everyone to the last moment. There is reason to believe that vaccination has preserved thousands who, from weak

constitutions, would have succumbed to smallpox. Thus the weak members of civilized societies propagate their kind. No one who has attended to the breeding of domestic animals will doubt that this must be highly injurious to the race of man" (emphasis is mine, PJW).

Dr. Woolsey Teller, founder of the American Association for the Advancement of Atheism, says: "Someday, when the world gets wiser than it is today, it may take up selective breeding of humans" *(Bales-Teller Debate)*.

Dr. George Simpson in his book *Meaning of Evolution* (333) says: "The means of biological evolutionary progress are already becoming clear, although it is doubtful whether we are ready yet to apply them well" ... he goes on to show that selective breeding is one of those methods.

Let the implications of such statements sink in! All of the sickening cruelty of heathen societies' "survival of the fittest," all of the stench of Hitler's "Master Race" ovens, are wrapped up in these conclusions. Some evolutionists may say that they are not willing to go that far ... but why not? If man is just a superior form of animal life, why not allow selective breeding to improve the strain? Why should moral, religious, and sociological factors even enter into the picture? One of the hardest questions for the evolutionist is this: "If man is just a higher animal, why is it wrong to kill a man but not wrong to kill a deer or chicken?"

IV. The Alternative Cannot Be Proved.
   A. Psalm 14:1 – "The fool hath said in his heart, there is no God." Why?
      1. Because he must deny his own nature and relegate himself to the level of brute animals.
      2. Because he closes his mind to all the evidence God has written into His creation.
      3. Because, from a logical and scientific standpoint, he is utterly unequipped to make such a declaration and incapable of proving it.
      4. To make such a declaration, one would have to possess the qualities of God.
         a. He would have to be omnipresent (everywhere in the Universe) because where he is not, God might be.
         b. He would have to be omniscient (know everything) because the truth he admits he does not know could be the proof that demonstrates the existence of God. He would have to be able, with certainty, to give a reason or cause for everything in the Universe or else that cause which he cannot describe may be God.
         c. He would have to be eternal because before he lived, God may have powerfully demonstrated His existence.
      5. In short, the presumption of this finite being – whose life span is just a dot on the pages of eternity, who knows only one little section on one little planet in a vast Universe, who is hedged about by inscrutable mysteries, who cannot say for sure where he came from, where he is going, or even if he will be here tomorrow – in making such a declaration is nothing short of amazing.

6. Of the three positions relative to the proposition that we mentioned in the beginning, we have seen that atheism is incapable of proof.
B. Agnosticism is unworthy of our notice.
 1. They freely admit, "We do not know." Why then give up a faith that is meaningful, a moral standard that is uplifting, a hope that sustains us in the trials and sorrows of life, the fellowship of the best people on earth when the best alternative is, "I do not know!"
C. That leaves theism, the belief that "God Is" as the most reasonable explanation for:
 1. The order, design, and purpose of this vast Universe.
 2. The origin and personality (intellect, moral consciousness, religious intuition, etc.) of man.
 3. Psalm 104:24: "O Lord, how manifold are Thy works. In wisdom has Thou made them all; the earth is full of Thy riches."

    Isaiah 40:25, 26: "To whom then will ye liken me that I should be equal to him? saith the Holy One. Lift up your eyes on high, and see who created these, that bringeth out their host by number...."

    Nehemiah 9:6: "Thou, even Thou, art Lord alone; Thou hast made heaven, the heaven of heavens with all their host, the earth and all things that are therein."

NOTES

The Bible: God's Word
2 TIMOTHY 3:16-17

God
Infinite
Omniscient

Revelation

Bible
Inspired

Intuition
Human Wisdom

Man
Finite
Limited

Revelation
1. Meaning of term
2. Necessity
3. Possible and Probable
4. Can We Understand It?
5. Can We Prove Anything by It?

Proofs of Inspiration
1. Unity
2. Fulfilled Prophecy
3. Archaeological
4. Accuracy
5. Pre-scientific
6. Style

Lesson 3

The Bible: God's Word

Introduction:
A. Review material on Chart 1 briefly.
   1. There is a God.
   2. God created man.
B. Our proposition in this lesson is that, having made man in his image (having intellect, wisdom, judgment, moral consciousness, etc.), God has revealed Himself and His will to man and that the Bible is that revelation.

I. Meaning of Revelation.

A. 2 Timothy 3:16, 17; 2 Peter 1:20, 21.
   1. The claim made here is that the Scriptures are "God breathed" or inspired and that they came not from human impulse or human wisdom.
B. "Reveal" – (W. E. Vine, *Expository Dictionary of New Testament Words*) – *apokalupto* is to uncover, unveil – something presented to the mind directly as the character of God as Father (Matt. 11:27), the will of God for the conduct of his children (Phil. 3:15), the mind of God to the prophets of Israel (1 Pet. 1:12) and to the church (Eph. 3:5).
C. Revelation (*Thayer's Greek-English Lexicon*, 62).
   1. "A laying bare, making naked."
   2. In New Testament, a disclosure of truth, instruction concerning divine things before unknown especially those relating to the Christian salvation given to the soul by God Himself or by the ascended Christ through the operation of the Holy Spirit (1 Cor. 2:10.)
D. Man's limitation constituted the main covering (Isa. 55:8, 9).
   1. God is infinite (without limitation).
      a. He is omniscient; He knows everything (Heb. 4:13.)
      b. He is omnipotent; He has all power (Mark 10:27).
      c. He is omnipresent; He is everywhere (Psa. 139:7-10).
   2. Man is finite (having bounds or limitations as to space, time, circumstances, etc.).
      a. He is limited in knowledge. (Jas. 4:14 – "whereas ye know not what shall be on the morrow.")
      b. He is limited in time. (Jas. 4:14 – "what is your life? It is even a vapor that appeareth for a little time and then vanisheth away.")
   3. Therefore, God's revelation had to remove the covering (man's limitation) and bridge the gap between human wisdom and divine wisdom, to light up the darkness, to draw back the veil and to show man what he is, where he came from, what he is here for, what his moral obligations are, and what his destiny is. (For full discussion on this point see *Ancient Faith in Conflict*, lecture on revelation by Pat Hardeman.)

II. The Necessity of a Revelation

A. Without a revelation from God to man, man by his own wisdom and resources could never have known God and His will for man.
   1. We cannot know God by nature.
      a. It is true that the "heavens declare the glory of God and the firmament showeth his handiwork" (Psa. 19:1-4; Rom. 1:20). As stated in the first lesson, the design and perfection of the universe certainly speaks to us of a designer. However, we can never know God, His

nature, His will for man, etc., by this means.
        b. From his earliest history man, with all his wisdom and all of his observation of nature, has worshiped the creature rather than the creator (Rom. 1:25). His gods have had no higher standard of morality than he has. His religious worship has simply made provision for his own lusts and appetites. The God of heaven has to all such been worshiped as an "unknown God" (Acts 17:23).
    2. We cannot know God by intuition.
        a. Some feel that we have some "inner light" that instructs and guides us.
        b. Jeremiah 10:23 and Proverbs 16:25 show that man is utterly incapable to direct his own steps.
        c. If we do have such an "inner light" or intuition, why do we need Christ or the Gospel? Why are there not churches springing up spontaneously all over the world separate and apart from the preaching of the Gospel?
    3. We cannot know God by human wisdom.
        a. 1 Corinthians 1:21; 3:19.
        b. Jeremiah 8:9.
        c. With all the vaunted accomplishments of the Roman Empire, with all the celebrated philosophers of Greece (Socrates, Aristotle, Plato, etc.), the moral and spiritual degradation of that generation is graphically pictured in Romans 1. Even Plato himself realized the inadequacy and limitation of human philosophy and human wisdom when he said late in life, "We will wait for one, either God or a God inspired man to teach us our religious duties and to take away the darkness from our eyes."
    4. Therefore, since man was utterly incapable of knowing the mind and will of God through his own devices, it was necessary for God to draw back the veil and dispel the darkness.

III. The Possibility and Probability of a Revelation

A. Granting the premise that there is a God who created the earth and man in his image, the following propositions ought to be self-evident:
    1. It was possible for God to reveal His will to men (Mark 10:27; Luke 1:37).
    2. It was probable that he would do so.
        a. God being grieved and offended by our sins would logically want to show us a better way.
        b. God, as our Father, would want to communicate with His children as surely as any parent would communicate with theirs.
        c. Man is inherently religious. To create man with a natural desire and thirst for spiritual things and to fail to provide a revelation to satisfy that desire and to direct it into proper channels would be as unreasonable as creating an eye without light or an ear without sound.

IV. Can We Understand This Revelation?

A. There is a prevalent idea in the world that we cannot understand the Bible.
    1. The Catholic position as stated by Cardinal Gibbons in *Faith of our Fathers* (94th Ed.; 89-90): "We must therefore conclude that the scriptures alone cannot be a sufficient guide and rule of faith

because they cannot, at any time, be within the reach of every inquirer, because they are not of themselves intelligible even in matters of highest importance, and because they do not contain all the truths necessary for salvation."
  2. The Denominational attitude is that creeds must be written to explain and interpret the Bible and that an educated "Clergy" must break it down and explain it to the "laity."
B. Review the purpose and meaning of revelation.
  1. To "reveal," "uncover," "lay bare" His mind, "to make manifest," to "declare" His will – this was God's avowed intention in this revelation.
     a. Isaiah 55:11 – "so shall my word be that goeth forth out of my mouth, it shall not return unto me void but it shall accomplish that which I please and it shall prosper in the thing whereunto I send it" (emphasis mine, PJW).
     b. If we cannot understand it, then God failed in His desire and His power is limited. Who is willing to accept such a conclusion?
  2. Why do you speak to anybody if not for the purpose of being understood? To contradict this is to accuse God of the worst possible deceit.
  3. God promises that we can understand His revelation.
     a. Matthew 5:6 – "Shall be filled."
     b. Matthew 13:15 – Jesus predicated salvation on hearing, understanding, and turning.
     c. John 6:44, 45.
     d. John 7:17.
     e. John. 8:32 – "ye shall know the truth."
     f. John 12:48 – even man's wisdom recognizes that a law that cannot be understood is an unjust law.
     g. Ephesians 3:3-5 – "ye may understand."
     h. Ephesians 5:17 – "Be not foolish but understand."
     i. 2 Timothy 3:15-16.
  4. Objections considered.
     a. "Doesn't the Bible claim to be a mystery?"
        (1) The term "mystery" in the New Testament does not mean something that cannot be understood but rather something that has been hitherto covered or not revealed.
        (2) The term "mystery" in the New Testament has reference to the Old Testament, not to the revelation of Christ given through the Apostles. In fact, wherever you find the term "mystery" in the New Testament, you find an accompanying phrase such as "revealed," "declared," "made known," "manifested," to show that these former mysteries are now revealed through the Apostles (Rom. 16:25, 26: Eph. 3:3-5; Col. 1:25, 26; 1 Cor. 2:6-10).
     b. "Isn't it true that you can prove anything by the Bible?"
        (1) No, it is not true. This is a blasphemous and wicked charge! To say you can prove any thing by John Doe (or anyone else) is to accuse him of deceit and duplicity.
        (2) Such is not true of the writings of men. Take a textbook on mathematics and try to prove that $2 \times 2 = 4$ and also that $2 \times 2 = 5$.

NOTES

(3) Such a charge makes God dishonest, the Bible inferior to the writings of men, and the whole idea of revelation a farce.

V. Proofs of Inspiration
- A. Unity.
  1. Not one, but 66 books written by about 40 men over a period of approximately 1500 years. The authors had different backgrounds, spoke several different languages, lived in different areas, yet their writings make a complete and harmonious whole. There are links or threads of evidence (messianic, historical, prophetic, and redemptive) that tie all of these books together and prove that they all stemmed from one mind, the mind of God.
- B. Fulfilled Prophecy. (For full discussion of fulfilled prophecy, see Bishop Newton on the *Prophecies*; *Prophecies Unveiled* by Morris, and *Divine Demonstration*, Everest, 282-355.)
  1. The prophecies of the Old Testament, written hundreds of years in advance of the events foretold, containing details that would be beyond the scope of human speculation, yet fulfilled in minute detail, constitute one of the strongest proofs of the inspiration of he Bible.
     a. God declared that such evidence is a proof of His superiority over men and all heathen gods (Isa. 41:1-8, 21-27; 42:8, 9; 46:8-11.)
  2. Some examples of fulfilled prophecy.
     a. Messianic prophecies. We will reserve our discussion of this spectacular demonstration of prophecy until next lesson.
     b. Noah's prophecy (Gen. 9:25-27).
        (1) "Cursed be (the father) of Canaan, of the descendants of Ham, a servant of servants shall he be unto his brethren."
            (a) Not a judgment from heaven but a prediction of what would be.
            (b) Sodom and Gomorrah, Tyre and Sidon, Egypt all visited with wrath and destruction. Africa is still the dark continent and still the arena for violence and terror.
            (c) It is an historical fact that many nations obtained their slaves from these people.
        (2) "Blessed of Jehovah, my God, be Shem – God will dwell in the tents of Shem."
            (a) The descendants of Shem, the Jewish Nation were the recipients of great privileges and blessings from Jehovah. Paul sums up these blessings in Romans 9:4, 5: "who are Israelites; whose is the adoption, and the glory, and the covenants, and the giving of the law, and the services of God, and the promises; whose are the fathers, and of whom is Christ as concerning the flesh... ."
        (3) "God shall enlarge Japheth."
            (a) He had more children; the races that trace their origin to him far outnumber the others.
            (b) He occupied greater territory.
                (i) The Hamite Nations remained fairly stable in the area of Africa.
                (ii) The Shemite Nations occupied Asia Minor.

NOTES

(iii) The Japhite Nations spread to the rest of the world, Europe, the Far East, America, etc.
   c. Prophecy concerning Ishmael (Gen. 16:10-12; 17:20.)
      (1) "Twelve princes shall he beget."
         (a) Listed in Genesis 25:12-17.
         (b) As late as A. D. 350, historians mention Arabs still governed by twelve princes.
      (2) "I will multiply thy descendants exceedingly."
         (a) The Itureans, the Arabs, the Saracens were all Ishmaelites. The Saracens indeed became a "great nation," gaining possession of nearly the whole civilized world.
      (3) "And he will be a wild man."
         (a) It has been characteristic of the Arabs to be wild, fierce, roaming the desert, plundering, etc.
      (4) "His hand will be against every man and every man's hand against him."
         (a) The plundering and murder that have characterized the Arab's attitude toward other peoples have naturally developed a hostility between other nations and them.
      (5) "And he shall tabernacle in the presence of his brethren."
         (a) The Arabs have dwelt in immediate proximity to the other descendants of Abraham – the Jews. Every effort by the Egyptians, the Assyrians, the Romans, the Greeks, and others to conquer them or assimilate them into their culture has failed.
   d. Baalam's prophecy concerning Israel (Num. 23 and 24).
      (1) "So the people shall dwell alone and shall not be reckoned among the nations" (23:9).
         (a) They did dwell alone, alone in a country isolated from other nations, alone in their customs and religious institutions, and alone in their refusal to mix and mingle with other peoples.
      (2) Israel was to become a great people; "who can count the dust of Jacob and number the fourth part of Israel?" (v. 10).
         (a) This, like the similar promise to Abraham in Genesis 12:3, was fulfilled as the Jews under David and Solomon became a great nation.
      (3) There would arise a "star out of Jacob and a sceptre shall rise out of Israel" – an eminent and powerful king should appear who would conquer Moab, Edom, and Amalek (24:17-18).
         (a) David was a "star" of the first magnitude, a great and powerful king. He did conquer the Moabites, Edomites, and Amalekites (2 Sam. 8.)
      (4) Asshur (Assyria) would carry Israel into captivity (Num. 24:22).
         (a) Fulfilled in 2 Kings 17, where It is mentioned that this had been foretold by the prophets.
   e. Prophecy concerning Israel's downfall (Deut. 28:14-64).
      (1) Foretold 400 years in advance that they should have a king (v. 36).
      (2) They would become a "hiss and a byword" (v. 37; Jer. 29:18).

NOTES

(3) The Lord would bring a nation whose language they did not understand (vv. 49, 50). Assyria, Babylon, and Rome all conquered the Jews.
(4) They would besiege Judea and Jerusalem, tear down their walls of protection, and the siege would become so severe that they would resort to cannibalism, eating their own children (vv. 49-57). This was literally fulfilled both in the Syrian siege (2 Kings 6:24-31) and the Roman destruction of Jerusalem in A. D. 70 (Josephus Book 6, Ch. 3, p. 818).
(5) Great numbers would perish making this great people few in number (v. 62). Josephus states that 1,240,000 Jews were slain in the destruction of Jerusalem.
(6) Many would be sold into slavery in Egypt (v. 68). This was fulfilled in Hosea 8:13 and in the destruction of Jerusalem where Josephus tells us that 99,200 prisoners were sold into slavery.
    f. Prophecies concerning other nations.
       (1) Fall of Babylon (Isa. 13:19-22; 14; Jer. 50).
       (2) Fall of Egypt (Isa. 19; Ezek. 29:30).
       (3) Fall of Nineveh (Book of Nahum; Zeph. 2:13-15; Isa. 10:12-14).
       (4) Fall of Tyre (Isa. 23; Ezek. 26: 27, 28; Zech. 9:3, 4).
       (5) Fall of Sidon (Ezek. 28:20-24).
       Thus we see that the history and downfall of nations were written hundreds of years before the events took place in amazing detail.

C. Archaeological proofs of inspiration.

(Scientists digging into the ruins of ancient cities having uncovered amazing corroborative evidence to verify the Bible account. Following are some of the results of such discoveries).

1. General Corroboration.
   a. Common origin of civilization – the tracing of all nations, domesticated plants and animals, back to the Tigris-Euphrates Valley.
   b. Connection of Jewish history with other nations such as Egypt, Philistines, Assyria, Babylon, etc. (The uncovering of battle records, names of kings, cities, etc., all fit in with the Bible account.)
2. Special Corroboration.
   a. Original monotheism (belief in one God), creation of world and man, fall of man.
      (1) The writings, seals, earliest records of all ancient civilization have borne out Bible story (Halley, 69-70).
   b. Early writing. Until fairly recent times, it was thought that writing was not known until the time of Moses. The Code of Hammurabi, the Weld Prism, the pre-flood tablets have now proven the use of writing in Abraham's day and even much earlier.
   c. Early use of metals (Gen. 4:21, 22). Until recently the "Iron Age" was supposed to be from 1200 B.C. onward. Dr. Frankfort's discovery in 1933 pushed the use of iron back 1500 more years. Other discoveries show use of bronze and other metals before the flood.
   d. Flood – confirmed by British Museum expedition 1929.
   e. Famine in Egypt in time of Joseph – confirmed by Petrie (1912).

f. Walls of Jericho – confirmed in amazing detail by Garstang (1929-36).
g. Solomon's wealth – stables, etc., uncovered by Oriental Institute (1939).
h. Building of Egyptian cities, Pithom and Raamses, by Hebrew slave labor (Exod. 1:11) – confirmed by Naville, 1883; Petrie, 1905; and Fisher, 1922.
i. Bricks without straw (Exod. 5) – confirmed by Kyle, 1908 who found at Pithom the lower courses of bricks filled with good straw, the middle courses with stubble, and the upper courses with no straw at all.
j. King Belshazzar of Babylon (Dan. 5). For many years all Babylonian records showed no such name listing Nabonidus as the last king before the Persian invasion. However, the British Museum discovered a number of clay tablets that listed Nabonidus as having a son, Belshazzar, who ruled jointly with him and was killed In the Persian conquest.

D. Scientific accuracy as a proof of inspiration.
1. Although admitted to be at least 1900 years old, the Bible contains none of the geographical, historical, and scientific mistakes and inaccuracies that characterize the writings of men. Books of medicine, astronomy, geology, etc., even 50 or 100 years old are usually outdated because of mistakes. Yet, here is a book that touches on all the known sciences and has no such inaccuracies.
2. Experts in these various fields have perused the Bible with extreme care and yet have failed to find any concrete example of error.

E. Pre-scientific knowledge as a proof of inspiration.
1. Scientific truths that were undiscovered by man with all his wisdom and resources are stated as facts hundreds of years in advance of the discovery of these truths by men.
   a. A few examples of such evidence.
      (1) Rotundity of the earth (Isa. 40:22; Luke 17:26).
      (2) Suspension of the earth in space (Job 26:7).
      (3) Empty space in the North (Job 26:7).
      (4) Static electricity (lightning) (Jer. 10:13).
      (5) Oceanography (paths in the seas) (Psa. 8).
      (6) Life In the blood (Lev. 17:10-16).
      (7) All nations of one blood (Acts 17:26).
      (8) Quarantine, disinfection procedures, covering over mouth in treatment of infectious diseases (Lev. 13 & 14).
      (9) Number of stars (Gen. 13:16; 15:5). (Ptolemy as late as 150 A. D. listed only 3,000.)
      (10) Process of rain, evaporation into air, and condensation to earth again (Eccl. 1:72; Job 36:27, 28).
      (11) Dimensions of ark (Gen. 6:15). (Modern ship builders still use the same ratio.)
      (12) Progression and classification of life – vegetable, fish, fowl, mammals, and man (Gen. 1).
      (13) Five facts of science (Gen. 1:1, 2).
         (a) "In the beginning" – time.

NOTES

- (b) "God created the heaven" – space.
- (c) "and the earth" – matter.
- (d) "and the Spirit of God" – force.
- (e) "moved upon the face of the waters" – motion.
  (Note: Since writing this I have come across an excellent study of the pre-scientific information in the Bible by brother A. O. Schnabel, a scientist for Boeing Aircraft Co. in Seattle, Washington.)

F. The style of the Bible as proof of inspiration.
   1. The amazing calmness and brevity of the Bible in recording the most stupendous events and tragedies is unlike anything written by men.
      a. Examples:
         (1) Creation of world and man – two chapters.
         (2) Death of Christ – about eight chapters.
         (3) Flood – three chapters.
         (4) Destruction of Jerusalem – three chapters.
         (Compare this reserved calmness with the volumes written on the deaths of Lincoln, Kennedy, Churchill, or natural disasters such as floods, earthquakes, etc.)
   2. The complete impartiality of its writers is unlike human authors.
      a. The candid statement of the sins and frailties of even its great heroes is unique in the histories of the world. (Noah's drunkenness, Abraham's falsehood, Jacob's deceit, David's adultery, Peter's cowardice, Paul's blasphemy, etc.).

G. The moral standard of the Bible as proof of its inspiration.
   1. The Old Testament writers lived in a country surrounded by and influenced by heathen religions and immoral practices shocking to contemplate. The New Testament writers were surrounded by the immoralities and vices of pagan Rome and Greece. Yet the moral standards they set forth were far in advance of anything known to their generations.
      a. How can the skeptic account for the fact that the world's greatest literature and highest moral standard come not from the geniuses of Rome, the philosophers of Greece, or the scholars and moralists of today but from the minds of a handful of Jewish fishermen who never went to college and never had another book published? (Of course, the Christian's answer is that these unlearned men were inspired by God to reveal a moral standard that would uplift and ennoble mankind.)
   2. Christianity is the one moral standard that admits of universal application without destroying the world.
      a. Plato's *Republic* would give a rebirth to slavery and the brothel as an accepted institution.
      b. The Koran would replace a religion of love with cruelty and the female half of the world's population would sink to levels of slaves or even dogs.
   3. Compare the moral standards of countries where the Bible is taught and has free course with countries like Russia, China, India, Africa, etc., where the teaching of the Bible is stifled and restricted.

NOTES

H. Its survival as proof of its inspiration.
   1. Imagine the odds against the writings of a handful of unlearned Jews, in a captive Roman Province, surviving the persecutions of the Jewish authorities and pagan religions and the determined effort of the Roman Empire to stamp them out. Then to survive 1800 years of the onslaughts of skeptics and atheists, the compromises of disloyal friends, etc., and to be the best known, the most widely read, the best loved, and the most influential of all the writings of men is nothing short of a miracle.
I. The Bible is either the work of men or of God.
   1. If from God, all of these phenomena are easily understood and accounted for.
   2. If from men, a logical explanation must be given for all of these evidences.
   3. If from men, let us remember the kind of men involved:
      a. They would be wicked men, liars and cheats who were trying to foist off upon the world a book that they claim was from God.
      b. That such a course could bring them no worldly benefits makes them not only wicked but stupid.
      c. To say that these nameless cheats invented the character of Christ, wrote the Sermon on the Mount, gave to the world a gospel that has molded the lives of the best and purest people for 1900 years is the dilemma that faces the person who denies that the Bible is from God.

Jesus Christ: The Son of God
MATTHEW 22:42; 16:16-18

1. Proposition Defined
2. Facts Admitted
    a. He Lived
    b. In Palestine
    c. In First Century
    d. Was a Religious Teacher
3. Alternatives

Jesus: The Christ	Jesus: The Imposter
• Claims	• Ordinary Jew
• Virgin Birth	• Limited Education
• Prophecies	• Jewish Prejudices & Hatred
• Unnatural Sayings & Deeds	• Worldly Ambition
• Miracles	• A Conscious Liar & Fraud
• Resurrection	

Lesson 4

Jesus Christ: The Son of God

Introduction:
A. Review.
   1. Chart I – There is a God. He created the Universe. He created man in His image.
   2. Chart II – The Bible is God's revelation to man.
      a. Review meaning of revelation ("uncover").
      b. Show possibility and probability of such a revelation.
      c. Show that we can understand it.
      d. Briefly run through proofs of inspiration.
B. Our proposition in this lesson is that, having proved the Bible to be a revelation from God to man, the fundamental and basic affirmation of that revelation is true; namely, that Jesus Christ is the Son of God.

I. The Proposition Defined.

   A. Matthew 22:42; 16:16-18.
      1. "Jesus" – A common name worn by many then and now (Col. 4:11).
      2. "Christ" –
         a. Hebrew "the Messiah," the one prophesied about in all of the Old Testament.
         b. Greek "anointed," signifying His being chosen of God to be Prophet (Acts 3:22, 23), Priest (Heb. 8:1), and King (Rev. 17:14).
      3. "The Son of God" – Not just "a" son of God, as men and angels are called in the Scriptures (Job 38:7; John 1:12; 1 John 3:2), but in a special and exclusive sense. He is "the only begotten Son of God" (emphasis mine, PJW).
   B. The significance of the proposition.
      1. A matter of revelation. Men could not know by "flesh and blood" (human testimony and human wisdom) this great truth (Matt. 16:16-18; 1 Cor. 12:3).
      2. Declared publicly and audibly by God (Matt. 3:17).
      3. Declared by angels to Mary and Joseph (Luke 1:35; Matt. 1:21).
      4. It is the theme of New Testament preaching (Acts 2:36; 17:3; 1 Cor. 2:2).
      5. It is the foundation of the church (Matt. 16:16-18).
         Note – Those who apply this passage so as to make Peter the foundation ignore Paul's statement in 1 Corinthians 3:11 and the fact that Jesus, Paul, and Peter all apply the passages concerning a foundation in Isaiah 28:16 and Psalms 118:22 to Jesus, not to Peter. (See Matt. 21:42; Rom. 9:33; Acts 4:10, 11; 1 Pet. 2:4.)
      6. It is the reason for the New Testament Scriptures (John 20:31).
      7. You must believe and confess it in order to be saved (Rom. 10:9, 10; Acts 8:37, 38).

II. Facts Admitted by All.

   A. That Jesus lived.
      1. All writers, enemies and friends, Jewish, Roman, Greek, etc., treat Jesus as an historical character, not as a fictitious character.
   B. He lived in Palestine.
      1. All writers refer to Him as a Jew who lived in Palestine.
   C. He lived at the beginning of the 1st century.
      1. To determine when George Washington lived, you could trace historical references to him in each generation until about 1700. Before that, his name is not mentioned. Obviously, then, he

lived during the 18th century.
2. Likewise, there is historical reference to Jesus in each century and generation back to the first century. Before that, He is not mentioned (except in prophecy, as we will see later in the lesson).

D. He was a religious teacher.
1. All writers refer to him as a teacher of religion, the author of the Christian religion. Before He lived, the Christian religion did not exist; since He lived, it has always been here.

III. There Are But Two Alternatives.

A. That Jesus is the Son of God as He claimed, that He was born miraculously, that He fulfilled Old Testament prophecy, that His actions and attitudes were contrary to those of ordinary men, that He performed miracles, and that He was raised from the dead.

B. If He is not what He claimed, then He was just an ordinary man, a Jewish imposter, limited in knowledge, filled with all of the prejudices and hatreds so common to the Jews of that day, filled with vain worldly ambition, and in all of His activities a conscious and deliberate liar and fraud.

C. The third alternative imagined by many that He was neither the Son of God nor a conscious liar and imposter, but that he was a great philosopher, a genius in his day, a great and good man is ridiculous to contemplate. As we shall study in a moment, He made the most stupendous and grandiose claims of any man that ever lived. If He was not what He claimed to be, He knew that such claims were untrue when He made them and hence He would be an unmitigated liar and not a good man in any sense of the term.
1. Some have suggested the possibility that He may have been mentally unbalanced and had "illusions of grandeur." But look at His life! He was always calm, rational, the master of every situation. No insane person ever so acted! That the world's highest moral standard could come from the mind of a sick and demented Jew is incredible.

IV. Evidences that He Is the Son of God.

A. His Claims:
1. He claimed to be sinlessly perfect.
   a. He challenged men to convict Him of sin (John 8:46).
   b. His disciples said He was sinless (Heb. 4:15; 1 Pet. 2:22), yet made no such claim for themselves (Luke 5:8; 1 Tim. 1:15).
   c. His friends lived with Him constantly for more than three years and had every opportunity to observe His life, yet found no fault in Him. (Even the one who betrayed Him admitted that Christ was innocent, Matt. 27:4.)
   d. His enemies used every means, legal and illegal, to convict Him of a sin or crime yet even the Roman authority who sentenced Him to die (as a political expedient) admitted His innocence (Matt. 21:24).
   e. Such a claim would have been disastrous to an imposter or fraud. He would know that he could not hide his mistakes and human frailties. But Jesus made the claim, lived the part, and at the same time condemned self-righteousness.

2. He claimed to be equal with God.
   a. John 5:17, 18; 14:6-10.
   b. Jesus lived always with the calm assurance that He was the Son of God, that He had the attributes and prerogatives of God, that He came from the Father and would return to Him.
   c. What sinful human being, what Jew living in a decadent and ignorant generation would ever conceive that such a relationship could exist between God in Heaven and man on earth?
   d. What imposter or fraud would have made the claim knowing that it would mean certain punishment for blasphemy?
3. He claimed that He would rise from the dead.
   a. Luke 9:22; Matthew 12:40; 16:21.
   b. What would an imposter, seeking to establish a false religion and further his own ends, possibly hope to accomplish by such a claim? He would know that within three days after his death he would be proven to be a liar.
4. He claimed that all men everywhere should love and obey Him.
   a. Matthew 10:37; Mark 16:15, 16.
   b. What Jewish imposter would have ever conceived of the Great Commission? The Jews were bound up in national pride; they hated the Gentiles. That a world-embracing message of good will would come from the prejudiced mind of a Galilean peasant is incredible. (For a full discussion of the claims of Jesus, see Mark Hopkins, *Evidences of Christianity*, 217-237, and H. Hailey, *Internal Evidences*, 31-40).

B. The Virgin Birth.
   1. Isaiah chapters 7-9 record a prophetic picture of the Messiah under the figure of a child.
      a. Isaiah 7:14 – "Therefore the Lord himself will give you a sign. Behold a virgin shall conceive and bare a son and shall call his name Immanuel."
      b. Isaiah 8 – This child "Immanuel" is mentioned twice again.
      c. Isaiah 9:6 – "Unto us a child is born... ." What child? The one mentioned in Isaiah 7:14 – Immanuel.
      d. When Jesus was born, Matthew 1:22, 23 says that Isaiah 7:14 was fulfilled. Luke 1:32, 33 shows that Isaiah 9:6, 7 was fulfilled.
      e. It is obvious that one of the signs by which God would identify the Messiah is that He would be born of a virgin, a miraculous and supernatural event.
   2. Modernists today delight in ridiculing and rejecting the virgin birth. Harry Emersan Fosdick states, "Of course I do not believe in the virgin birth or in that old-fashioned doctrine of the atonement and I do not know any intelligent Christian minister who does."
      a. They say, "It is contrary to the natural law of procreation." Certainly it is, that's the point! It was a miraculous sign given by God. Surely He who could create both man and woman from the dust of the ground in the beginning could create life separate from His law again.
      b. To deny the virgin birth is to deny the validity of the Gospel records. Note Matthew's account, chapter 1:18-25.
         (1) v. 18 – "Before they came together" (or cohabited).

(2) v. 19 – Joseph knew the child was not his and would have put her away.
   (3) v. 20 – The angel said "that which is conceived in her is of the Holy Spirit."
   (4) v. 22 – Matthew says that it is a fulfillment of Isaiah 7:14.
   (5) v. 25 – Matthew states that "he knew her not till she had brought forth a son" (emphasis mine – PJW).
C. Fulfilled Prophecies.
   1. Jesus claimed that He was the fulfillment of the Messianic prophecies (John 5:39; Luke 24:25-27; 44).
   2. The apostles claimed these applied to Him (Acts 3:18; 10:43).
   3. Bear in mind that this was not an afterthought. Jesus made this claim while He was yet living.
   4. Examples of prophecies fulfilled.

Examples	Prophecy	Fulfilled
1. Born of Woman	Genesis 3:15	Galatians 4:4
2. Born of Virgin	Isaiah 7:14	Matthew 1:22
3. Lineage of Abraham	Genesis 12:3	Acts 3:25-26
4. Family of David	Psalm 132:11; Jeremiah 23:5	Matthew 1:1-2; 3:3
5. Time of Birth (Preceded by a Forerunner)	Isaiah 40:3; Malachi 3:1; 4:5	Matthew 3:3; Luke 3:3-4
6. Place of Birth	Micah 5:2	Matthew 2:5-6
7. Divinity	Psalm 2:7; Isaiah 9:6; 25:9; Jeremiah 23:6	Acts 13:33; Matthew 11:27; Luke 2:11
8. Slaughter of Babies	Jeremiah 31:15	Matthew 2:17-18
9. Galilean Ministry	Isaiah 9:1-2	Matthew 4:14-16
10. His Priesthood	Psalm 110:4; Zechariah 6:12-13	Hebrews 5:6; 7:17-21
11. To Be a Prophet	Deuteronomy 18: 15, 18	Acts 3:22
12. Purging the Temple	Psalm 69:9	John 2:17
13. Triumphant Entry	Isaiah 62:11; Zechariah 9:9	Matthew 21:4-5
14. Betrayed by a Friend	Psalm 41:9; 55:13	John 13:18
15. Price of Betrayal	Zechariah 11:12-13	Matthew 27:9-10
16. Deserted by Disciples	Zechariah 13:7	Matthew 26:56
17. Silent Before Accusers	Psalm 38:13-14; Isaiah 53:7	Matthew 27:12-14
18. Mocked and Insulted	Psalms 35:15-16; 22:7; 69:21	Matthew 26:67; 27:39-40
19. Vinegar and Gall	Psalm 69:21	Matthew 27:34; John 19:29-30
20. Cries on the Cross	Psalms 22:1; 31:5	Matthew 27:46
21. Vicarious Death	Isaiah 53:4, 6	Matthew 8:17
22. Crucified Among Thieves	Isaiah 53:12	Matthew 27:58
23. Nailed – Pierced	Psalm 22:16; Zechariah 12:10	John 19:34, 37
24. No Bones Broken	Psalm 34:20	John 19:33, 36
25. Casting Lots for Garments	Psalm 22:18	John 19:23-24
26. Grave with the Rich	Isaiah 53:9	Matthew 27:57-60
27. Resurrection	Psalm 16:10; 30:30	Acts 2:31-32
28. Coronation	Psalms 110:1-2; 24:7-10	Acts 1:9; Ephesians 1:20-23

5. Suppose you read a book in a library about a man from a large family, whose father was United States Ambassador to England, whose oldest brother was killed in World War II, who piloted a P. T. Boat for the U. S. Navy, who was a senator from Massachusetts, who became the first Catholic President of the United States, and who was assassinated in Dallas, Texas. You would immediately recognize that these facts apply to only one man, John F. Kennedy. Now suppose that the librarian proved to you that the book was printed in 1700. Imagine, a man's whole life portrayed in detail and in print hundreds of years before he was ever born! Yet that is exactly what you have in these Messianic prophecies. These prophecies were all recorded and in a complete translation in the Greek language (Septuagint Version) at least 250 years before Jesus was born.
6. Now what could a Jewish imposter, a fraud trying to begin a new sect, possibly hope to gain by making such a claim? Even if he were foolish enough to read those prophecies and decide to play the part, there would be things over which he would have no control (where he would be born, the amount of money paid for his betrayal, the events of his death, the disposition of his garments after death, etc.)

D. Unnatural Sayings and Deeds.
1. Read the accounts of Jesus's earthly life as recorded in the Gospel record, study carefully His teaching and His actions and ask yourself, "Are these the actions and sayings of a natural man? Did He react to situations as men do today? Would a Jewish imposter, a cheat, and a fraud have so acted?"
2. Some unnatural attitudes of Jesus:
   a. He was completely devoid of worldly ambition.
      (1) When they tried to make Him a worldly king, He refused (John 6:15).
      (2) When a rich ruler came to Him, who could have helped Him advance His cause, He sent him away by imposing upon him a condition that the rich could not accept (Mark 10:17-22).
      (3) Whereas a Jewish fraud trying to establish a religion would naturally try to influence and win the support of the rulers, the chief priests, and the scribes, Jesus cultivated the poor and the sinners (Luke 15:1, 2) and rebuked the ones in prominent positions (Matt. 23).
   b. He never expressed a doubt on any subject (John 7:46).
      (1) He did not admit ignorance of anything; to Him there were no mysteries; He spoke as One who possessed all truth. He never appealed to human philosophy or human authority in an attempt to bolster his arguments. He did not apologize for even the most revolutionary statements, nor did He burden them with complicated or wordy explanations. His authority did not come from education, political influence, popularity, or any such source, but was inherent within Him (Matt. 7:29).
   c. He was entirely free of prejudice or hatred.
      (1) While surrounded by prevailing prejudices against the Gentiles (John 4:9), He treated all kindly and in the religion He established, made Jew and Gentile, slave and free,

male and female, equal (Mark 16:15, 16; Gal. 3:28, 29). What Jewish fraud would have so acted?
- d. He was entirely fearless and set forth teachings that were certain to bring persecution.
  - (1) While all Jews looked with pride upon Jerusalem as the chosen city of God, the center of a physical kingdom to come, Jesus plainly foretold its utter destruction (Matt. 24).
  - (2) While the Jews looked upon the Ten Commandments, the law of Moses, as the ultimate and eternal law, Jesus taught that it was to be abrogated and that men were to hear Him rather than Moses (Matt. 5; Col. 2:14).
  - (3) While the Jewish nation looked for a worldly Messiah to set up an earthly kingdom, He said, "My kingdom is not of this world" (John 18:36).
  - (4) What Jewish imposter, seeking to establish a new religion would have made such statements calculated to bring the wrath of the Jewish people down upon him? What would He have to gain by condemning all of the existing Jewish sects, showing disregard for their vaunted traditions, and accusing their leaders of hypocrisy?
- e. He had no malice or ill-will even toward His enemies (Matt. 5:44). His statement as He hung dying on the cross is not the statement of a human being whose earthly plans had been frustrated and defeated (Luke 23:34).
- f. He was entirely free of egotism and selfishness.
  - (1) Scrutinize carefully the life of Jesus and see if you can find one selfish thing that He ever did. His whole life was spent in service and sacrifice for others (Matt. 20:27, 28).
  - (2) What egotist, what Jewish imposter seeking to gather support for himself, would ever have spoken as Jesus did in giving God all the credit for what He accomplished (John 5:30; 11:40-43; 12:48, 49)?
  - (3) Some unnatural sayings of Jesus:
    - (a) John 8:58. What Jew living in that day would have conceived of a pre-existence?
    - (b) Matthew 24:35. From a human being, the statement that his words were of such import that they would outlast all the teachings of all other men but would outlast the Universe itself, would be the height of audacity.
    - (c) John 5:22, 26, 27; 12:48. For one who taught others, "Judge not lest ye be judged," these statements are nothing short of amazing.
    - (d) Matthew 4:10; John 4:23, 24. While claiming that only God should be worshiped, He accepted worship from many people (Matt. 8:2, 9:18; John 9:35-38; Matt. 28:9; John 20:26-29).
    - (e) John 5:21, 28, 29. What human being would ever risk the ridicule and exposure that could come from falsely claiming to rise from the dead? (For full discussion on these points, see Mark Hopkins, *Evidences*, 210-237 and Foy E. Wallace, Jr., *Bulwarks of the Faith*, II: 321-326.)

E. Miracles of Jesus.
  1. What is a miracle?
     a. A miracle is the direct intervention of God in the affairs of men, an event that indicates the presence or sanction of Deity, an event not brought about by the ordinary forces of nature

or by ordinary men.
2. Are miracles possible?
   a. Admit the existence of God and all things are possible to such an omnipotent power. If we believe the first verse of the Bible, our faith ought not to waver at any miracle therein.
3. What purpose do miracles serve?
   a. "There is one great purpose which is assigned to miracles, viz., the proof of a revelation, and certainly if it was the will of God to give a revelation, there are plain and obvious reasons for asserting that miracles are necessary as the guarantee and voucher for that revelation. A revelation is, properly speaking, such only by virtue of telling us something that we could not know without it. But how do we know that that communication of what is undiscoverable by human reason is true? Our reason cannot prove the truth of it; for it is by the supposition beyond our reason. There must be, then, some note or sign to certify to it and to distinguish it as a true communication from God, which note can be nothing else than a miracle" (A. B. Bruce, *Chief End of Revelation*, 162).
   b. Jesus claimed that the miracles He performed were God's stamp of approval upon Him as God's revelation to man (John 5:36; 10:25; Matt. 11:2-6).
4. Did Jesus actually perform miracles?
   a. He said He did (John 5:36; 10:25; Matt. 11:2-6).
   b. His disciples said He did (Acts 2:22; John 3:2).
   c. His enemies said that both He and His disciples did (Matt. 12:22-24; Acts 4:10, 16).
   d. The Bible records them as facts. To deny miracles is to deny the inspiration of the Bible (see proofs of inspiration in previous lesson).
   e. Historians say that He did. Josephus describes Him as "a doer of wonderful works."
   f. It was 100 years or more after the death of Christ before anyone attempted to deny His miracles as valid.
5. To even claim such miraculous power would have been disastrous for a Jew trying to usurp authority and establish a new religion. He would know that in those multitudes, and certainly among his followers, would be those who could disprove his claim.
   a. To say that Jesus succeeded by fakery and deceit to convince everybody, friends and foes alike, would make Him the greatest sleight of hand artist the world has ever known (as well as the biggest cheat).
   b. And even if you granted the inconceivable possibility of His fooling everybody by stupendous acts of legerdemain, how do you account for His failing to capitalize on the publicity? Why would He tell those who saw His magic to keep it quiet (Matt. 9:30; 12:16; 17:9; Mark 3:12; Luke 5:14; etc.)?
F. His resurrection.
1. We have already seen how utterly foolish it would have been for an imposter to claim that he would be raised from the dead. But Jesus made the claim repeatedly and His Apostles affirmed that they were witnesses of it.
2. The fact of the resurrection is the greatest proof of the Christian religion (Rom. 1:4; 1 Cor. 15:12-19).

NOTES

a. If we accept it as true, every claim and action of Jesus is verified.
b. If we reject it, Jesus as a good man, the Bible as a good book, Christianity as a worthwhile religion, are likewise cast aside.
3. The Apostles as witnesses of the resurrection.
   a. Their honesty, integrity, competency, etc. are unquestioned. They risked everything of a worldly nature, even their own lives, to proclaim this fact. The transformation in their lives following their seeing Jesus arisen from the dead is evidence of their firm conviction.
   b. They were sufficient in number to preclude any possibility of mistake.
4. Facts admitted by all:
   a. Jesus not only lived but was crucified by Jews and Romans.
   b. He was buried in a sealed tomb.
   c. His body disappeared.
5. Explanations given.
   a. The swoon theory (that Jesus was not actually dead, and that He revived from a state of unconsciousness and walked out of the tomb).
      (1) Does not account for soldier's actions (John 19:33).
      (2) Does not account for testimony of a competent Roman officer (Mark 15:44, 45).
      (3) Does not account for how those who worked on His body, anointed and wrapped it, etc., could have failed to perceive life in His body.
      (4) Does not account for how after such physical torture on the cross, plus a spear wound in His side with accompanying loss of blood, plus at least two days without food, water, or medication, He could undo the wrappings, take time to fold them neatly, roll away the huge stone at the entrance, fight off a Roman guard, walk the length of Palestine, and appear healthy and hearty to His disciples.
   b. The theory that the enemies of Jesus stole the body.
      (1) They had no motive! It would defeat their purpose. They wanted Him dead and buried and made every precaution to assure the body being still in the grave three days later (Matt. 27:62-66).
      (2) If they had, all they would have had to do on the day of Pentecost (Acts 2) would have been to produce the dead body of Jesus to forever put an end to His claims and His teaching.
   c. The theory that the disciples stole the body.
      (1) Does not account for how a guard of at least twelve Roman soldiers (under penalty of death if negligent) would allow the disciples to take the body.
      (2) Does not account for motive. The disciples dispersed after the crucifixion and did not expect Jesus to be raised. Would they have risked their lives, suffered persecution and privation for that which they knew was a lie?
   d. The "hallucination" theory. (That the disciples wanted to see Jesus so badly, they mistook a vision or dream for reality.)
      (1) Jesus corrected them when they at first thought they saw a vision (Luke 24:36, 37).
      (2) Thomas wanted proof positive (John 20:24-30).

NOTES

                    (3) The variety of appearances as to number and circumstances preclude the possibility.
                        (a) Not just one appearance but many, over a space of 40 days.
                        (b) Not just to one group but to groups of 2, 12, and even 500 at once.
                    (4) Besides the disciples were not expecting to see Him.
                    (5) Besides all that, if it had been an hallucination, the body would still have been in the tomb.
                c. That He arose from the dead!

Conclusion.

A. Take divinity away from Jesus and what do you have?
    1. A Jew born in a captive Roman province of a peasant woman lived as a carpenter's son for 30 years, became a teacher of religion for 3.5 years, was deserted by His followers when arrested, tried, and killed as a common criminal. He never wrote a book, never invented a machine, never went to college, yet He claims to be equal with God, to be the light of the world, that He would judge the world, that He would arise from the dead, and that He was sinless.
        a. More than that, He succeeded in having all time reckoned from Him (when we write A. D. 1967, we acknowledge His claim).
        b. He established a religion that has grown and spread throughout the whole world.
        c. More than that, this nameless cheat, this fraud, invented the character of Christ, and successfully played the part for a number of years!
        d. Though a conscious liar, He gave the world the highest moral standard it has ever known.
        e. Who can believe it? The only logical and rational conclusion to reach is that Jesus is what He claimed to be, the Christ and the Son of God!

NOTES

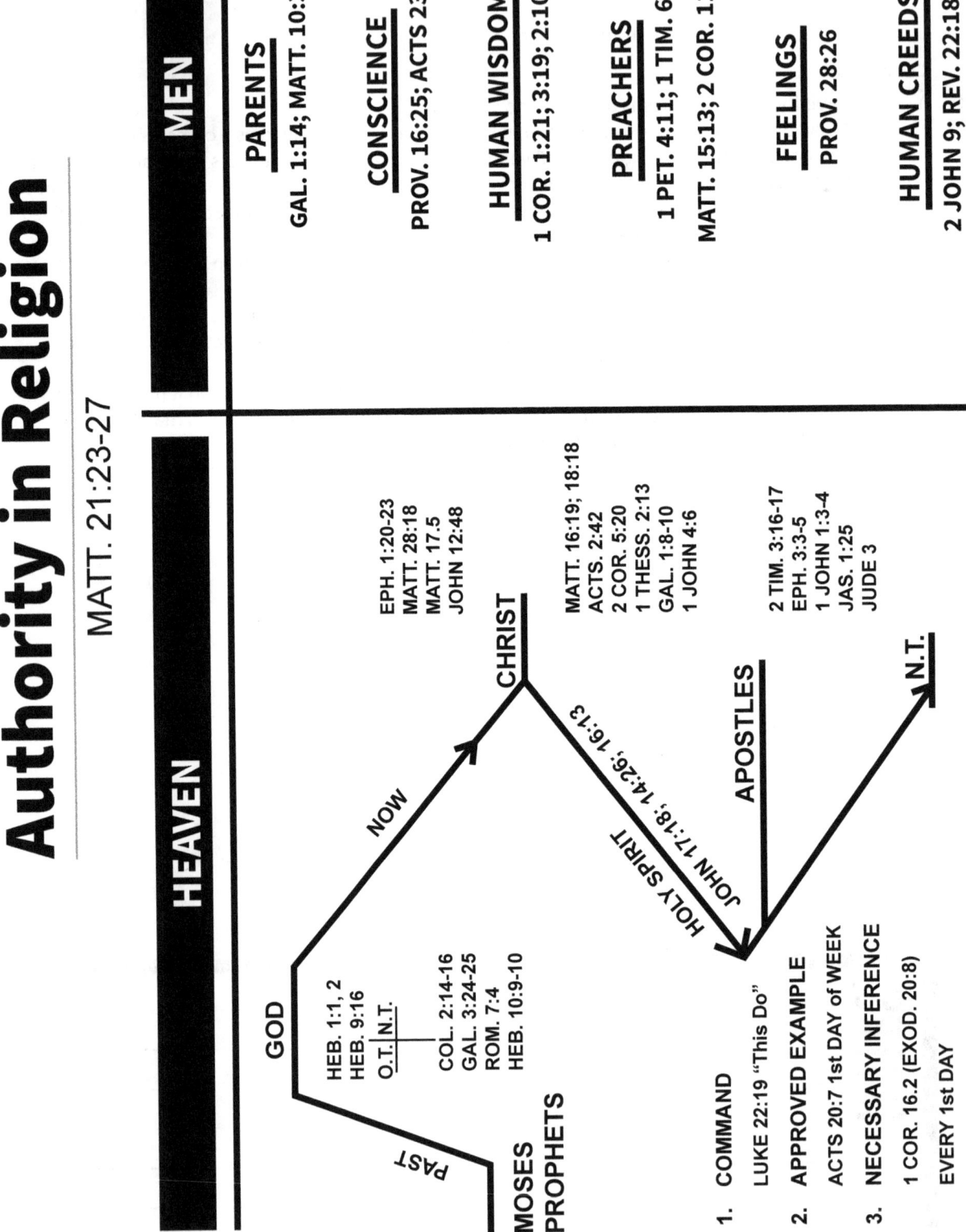

Lesson 5

Authority in Religion

Introduction:

A. Review previous lessons. Propositions established thus far:
1. There is a God.
2. God created man in His Image.
3. God revealed Himself and His will to man and that revelation is found in the Bible.
4. The fundamental truth of that revelation is that Jesus Christ is the Son of God.

I. **Meaning of, and Need for, Authority in Religion.**

   A. Definition – "legal or rightful power, dominion, a right to command" (Webster).

   B. In every realm of activity (the home, the school, the community, the Army, etc.) men recognize that some one must have legal or rightful power to rule and command and maintain law and order. The only alternative is lawlessness or anarchy.
   1. The need for standards of authority are recognized in all of the endeavors of men:
      a. Standards of weights and measures.
      b. Standards of time.
      c. Standards of quality in food and drugs.
      d. Standards for traffic speed and direction.
      e. Standards of monetary value.
   2. The confusion that would result from the elimination of such standards is obvious.

   C. Surely in the most important transaction of all, the salvation of our souls, there is a need for some standard of authority.
   1. One of the most confusing and backward periods in the history of the Jewish nation was described as entirely lacking in respect for God's standard of authority, "every man did that which was right in his own eyes" (Judg. 21:25– i.e., each one became a law unto himself).
   2. The division and confusion in the religious world today, with a multiplicity of conflicting churches and contradictory doctrines, can be directly related to a failure to recognize any single standard of authority in religion. Again, each one has become a law unto himself, or does "what is right in his own eyes," or as it is expressed today, "it doesn't make any difference what you believe as long as you're sincere."

   D. If God had not intended the spiritual realm to be one in which a single standard of authority is recognized and respected, He would never have used the figures "army," "body," "family," and "kingdom," to represent that realm. God commands that we all "speak the same thing" (1 Cor. 1:10, emphasis mine, PJW) and "that we all walk by the same rule" (Phil. 3:16). To find that standard or rule and to walk by it is one of man's greatest missions. Many will be rejected in the day of Judgment for lawlessness ("iniquity," without authority, Matt. 7:21-23).

   E. Jesus recognized only two general sources of authority in spiritual matters (Matt. 21:23-27).
   1. Despite the dilemma of the Jews, the answer was obvious. The baptism of John was from heaven (John 1:6; Matt. 3:14, 15; Luke 7:29, 30).
   2. But suppose it had not been from heaven – what is the only other alternative that Jesus recognized? If it had not come from heaven it would have come from men.
   3. "Is it from Heaven or Men?," "Does it rest upon Divine or Human authority?" – these are vital and practical questions relative to our religious beliefs and practices, the church of which we are a member, etc.

II. How Can We Know It Is from Heaven?

A. In order to be from Heaven it must originate with God.
   1. God is the source of truth (Jas. 1:17, 18; Isa. 46:9, 10).
   2. God has spoken to man (Heb. 1:1, 2).
      a. God's authority in times past (in the Jewish dispensation) was exercised in and through Moses and the Prophets and was directed to the Jewish fathers.
      b. God's authority "in these last days" (in the Christian dispensation) is exercised in and through Christ and is directed to "us."
      c. This eliminates Old Testament authority in religion today.
         (1) Hebrews 10:9-10 – One of the reasons Christ came was to:
             (a) Take away the Old Covenant.
             (b) Establish the New Covenant – "By the which will we are sanctified."
         (2) Hebrews 9:16-17 – In speaking of God's law as a will and testament, three facts are obvious:
             (a) Two wills and testaments cannot be in operation at the same time governing the same group of people (Heb. 10:9, 10).
             (b) The testament of Christ could not go into effect until He died.
             (c) Any hope we have of being heirs of Christ must be based upon compliance with the terms of His will.
         (3) Colossians 2:14-16.
             (a) Whatever law it was is said to be "nailed to the cross," "blotted out," "taken out of the way."
             (b) V. 16 – "let no man therefore judge you" about what? About the laws of meats, holy days, Sabbaths, etc., contained in the Old Testament.
         (4) Galatians 3:24-25.
             (a) The Law was our (Jews) schoolmaster to bring us unto Christ.
             (b) After faith is come (the gospel), we are no longer under the schoolmaster (or the Old Testament law).

B. In order to be from Heaven, it must come through Christ.
   1. Ephesians 1:20-23.
      a. The head directs and guides the movements of the body. The church has no right to teach or practice anything that the Head (Christ) does not direct.
      b. Any theory or system that denies that, from the time of His ascension, Jesus has had complete and final authority, is a false system ("Jehovah's Witnesses," Premillennialists, etc.).
   2. Matthew 28:18.
      a. "All Power" ("authority" ASV) means all legislative, executive, and judicial authority resides in Him.
   3. Matthew 17:5.
      a. The only subject of sufficient import to warrant God speaking directly and audibly to man was the authority of His Son.

NOTES

4. John 12:48.
    a. What more compelling incentive can we have to recognize and respect the authority of Christ than the realization that our lives will be judged by that standard?
C. In order to be from Heaven, it must come from Christ through His Apostles as they were guided by the Holy Spirit.
    1. John 17:18; 14:26; 16:13, 14.
        a. The revelation that God gave to His Son, Christ entrusted to His chosen Apostles and guarded the transmission of it by the Holy Spirit working in them.
        b. Jesus "sent" them into the world in the same sense in which God had "sent" Him into the world.
            (1) To reject Jesus is to reject God (1 John 2:23). To hear Jesus is to hear God (John 3:34; 12:49).
            (2) Likewise, to receive the Apostles is to receive the Christ who sent them (Matt. 10:40). To reject the Apostles is to reject Christ and God (1 John 4:6; John 3:34).
    2. Matthew 16:19; 18:18.
        a. The idea of "keys" has, in the Bible, the significance of power and authority.
            (1) The giving of "keys" to Christ signified His authority (Isa. 22:22; 9:6-7; Rev. 3:7).
            (2) Likewise the giving of "keys" to the Apostles signifies the delegation of authority from Christ to them.
    3. Acts 2:42.
        a. The standard of authority recognized and used by the early church was the "Apostles' doctrine." Of course we realize that this term is used because they revealed it, not that they invented it (Gal. 1:11, 12).
    4. 2 Corinthians 5:20.
        a. An ambassador is a personal representative speaking for another. They (the Apostles) came "in behalf of," "in the stead of," "in the name (or authority) of."
        b. For the Russian leader to slap the U. S. Ambassador in the face would be more than a personal insult; it would constitute a grievous affront to the U. S. Government whom he represents. Likewise to belittle and minimize the Apostles is a direct affront to God and Christ who sent them.
    5. 1 Thessalonians 2:13; Galatians 1.8-10; 1 John 4:6.
        a. To honor the word of the Apostles is to honor God. To preach anything based upon some other authority is to bring the anathema of God upon us.
        b. They constitute the Supreme Court of the Christian religion (Matt. 19:28); from their decisions there is no other source of appeal (Acts 15:6, 22-29).
D. In order to be from Heaven, it must be recorded in the writings of the Apostles, the New Testament.
    1. What the Apostles received by the Holy Spirit they wrote for all future generations (2 Pet. 3:1, 2; 1 John 1:3, 4; 1 Cor. 2:10-13; 14:37; Eph. 3:3-5).
    2. The completeness and sufficiency of that revelation is emphasized in the following passages: 2 Timothy 3:16, 17; 2 John 9; James 1:25; 2 Peter 1:3; John 16:13; Jude 3-5.

NOTES

a. Note especially the phrase "once for all" (Literally "one time for all time").
   (1) All of the sacrifice necessary to save man from sin was made by Christ "once for all" (Heb. 7:27; 9:28; 10:10). No additional sacrifice would ever have to be made!
   (2) All of the revelation necessary to teach and instruct man was given "once for all" to the saints of the 1st century (Jude 3, 5). No additional revelation would ever have to be made! (Not through the Pope, Joseph Smith, Mary B. Eddy, or anyone else.)
3. "How to Establish Authority from New Testament Scriptures" (From *Walking by Faith*, Roy Cogdill).
   a. By precept. By this we mean direct statement or positive command.
   b. By approved example. By this we mean the practice of the church in the New Testament under apostolic guidance and which the apostles received from the Lord and therefore by divine appointment.
   c. Necessary Inference. That which though neither expressly stated nor specifically exemplified yet is necessarily implied by the clear import and meaning of the language used.
      (1) These three methods of receiving divine authority illustrated by the Lord's Supper:

      PRECEPT
      (a) Its observance. "This do in remembrance of me" (1 Cor. 11:25).
         (i) Paul received it of the Lord and gave it to the church by His authority. Matthew 28:20 – "teaching them to observe all things whatsoever I have commanded" (1 Cor. 11:23).

      APPROVED EXAMPLE
      (b) The time of its observance, "and upon the first day of the week, when the disciples came together to break bread" (Acts 20:7).
         (ii) He remained in Troas for seven days – obviously waiting for the day upon which the saints assembled (Acts 20:7).
         (iii) This evidences that the Lord's Supper was observed in the church of the New Testament only upon the first day of the week – the Lord's day (Rev. 1:10).

      NECESSARY INFERENCE
      (c) The frequency of its observance. "The first day of the week to break bread."

      Compare:

      "Remember the Sabbath day to keep it holy" (Exod. 20:8).
      "The first day of the week to break bread" (Acts 20:7).
      NOTE: If "the Sabbath day to keep it holy" means every Sabbath day, as regularly as it comes, then "the first day of the week to break bread" means every "first day," as regularly as it comes. This is the "unavoidable implication of the clear import and meaning of the language used. There is no other way of determining how often this memorial supper is to be observed" (end of quote, PJW).
4. In order for a thing to be scriptural then it must be found in the New Testament Scriptures in one of the three ways mentioned.

a. Any doctrine that comes from some other source is condemned (2 John 9).
b. Any worship or service that is not enjoined by the Scriptures is will worship and will corrupt and make vain our worship (Matt. 15:9; John 4:24; Col. 2:20-23).
c. Any church whose name, doctrine, organization, work, worship, and terms of membership are not clearly stated in the Scriptures is not the Lord's church (Matt. 16:18; Rom. 16:16; Eph. 4:4, 5).
5. There are two general extremes in the application of these Scriptures to religious practice today.
    a. "Everything is acceptable as worship and service to God that is not specifically condemned." This is the attitude of denominationalism, the digressives, etc. It opens the door to counting beads in prayer, incense burning, foot washing, instrumental music, entertainment, etc.
    b. "Everything we use in carrying out the Lord's commands must be specifically mentioned or they are sinful." This is the position of the "one container"-for-the-Lord's-Supper brethren, the no-class brethren, the baptizing-in-running water advocates, and the upper-room advocates. This makes no provision for generic, or general authority (i.e., the use of any method or means of execution, in carrying out a command that is of the same class or order of the command and is not specifically commanded).

III. Sources of Human Authority (From Men)

A. Man has always been disposed to substitute his will for God's will and to turn from the authority of God to the authority of men (examples: Cain; Nadab and Abihu; King Saul; etc.). God's attitude toward such is vividly expressed in Jeremiah 2:13, "For my people have committed two evils; they have forsaken me, the fountain of living waters, and hewed them out cisterns, broken cisterns, that can hold no water" (see also Matt. 7:26, 27).
B. Let us consider some of the "broken cisterns" or "sand" that men are building their religious convictions and practices upon:
   1. Parents.
      a. Many are what they are and believe what they do for no better reason than that is the way they were raised – "If it's good enough for my parents, it's good enough for me!"
         (1) Saul of Tarsus had to forsake the religion of his parents (Gal. 1:14).
         (2) Matthew 10:37.
   2. Conscience.
      a. "Let your conscience be your guide" is the motto of many in religion.
         (1) Saul of Tarsus learned that this was not a sufficient guide (Acts 23:1; Prov. 16:25).
         (2) Conscience is that faculty of mind that tells us whether we are doing right or wrong according to the way we have been taught. But like a clock if it is set wrong, it will always be wrong no matter how well it operates.
   3. Human Wisdom.
      a. Many people in the religious world put their trust in, and build upon, the wisdom of the scholars of the religious world (1 Cor. 1:21; 2:5; 3:19; Jer. 8:9; 10:23).

NOTES

b. Many trust in another form of human wisdom, their own "think-so."
   (1) 1 Corinthians 2:10-14.
       (a) We cannot know what any man thinks unless he reveals it to us.
       (b) Likewise we cannot know what God thinks unless it is revealed to us by His Spirit in the Apostles.
       (c) Remember God said, "my thoughts are not your thoughts" (Isa. 55:8).
4. Preachers.
   a. The faith of many is built upon the "clergy" or "hierarchy." For example, the expression "I don't know, but my preacher can tell you."
      (1) Any preacher is a human authority unless he is citing divine authority for what he says (1 Tim. 6:3; 2 Cor. 11:14; Matt. 15:13; 1 Pet. 4:11).
5. Feelings.
   a. Many put their trust in some physical feeling "better felt than told."
   b. Feelings have to do with the physical nature while salvation has to do with our spiritual nature.
   c. Feelings can be very deceptive in religious matters (Gen. 37:29-36; Prov. 28:26).
6. Human Creeds.
   a. These are manuals, disciplines, catechisms, etc. that are supposed to summarize and explain what the New Testament teaches.
      (1) The argument of the pioneer preachers is still valid: "If the creed contains more than the New Testament it contains too much; if it contains less than the New Testament, it does not contain enough" (Rev. 22:18, 19; 2 John 9).

CONCLUSION:

Is your faith from heaven or men? Have you examined the church of which you are a member, what you believe and practice, etc., by the New Testament scriptures, rejecting everything that is not found in the inspired writings?

NOTES

Why You Need Christ
JOHN 14:16; 15:4-5

Man Needs	Jesus Is
1. An Object of Worship	Immanuel (God with us) (Matt. 1:23; Col. 2:9)
2. A Sacrifice for Sin	Lamb of God (John 1:29)
3. An Example of Manhood	Leader and Commander (Isa. 55:4; Heb. 2:10; 1 Pet. 2:21)
4. A Friend	A True Friend (Prov. 18:24; John 15:13)
5. A Hope	Our Hope (1 Tim. 1:1; Col. 1:27)
6. A Purpose in Life	The Way (John 14:6; Jer. 32:39)
7. Freedom	The Truth (John 14:6; 8:31-32; Rom. 11:26)
8. An Abundant Life	The Life (John 14:6; 10:10; 20:31)
9. Peace	Our Peace (Eph. 2:14; John 14:27; Phil. 4:7; John 16:33)
10. Health	Great Physician (Jer. 8:22; Mark 2:17)

Lesson 6

Why You Need Christ

Introduction:
A. Brief review of previous lessons.
B. One of the most impressive and unique things about the Bible and the Christ revealed in the Bible is the way in which Jesus supplies an answer for every problem and meets and satisfies every basic need of man (spiritual, moral, or psychological) (John 14:1-6; 15:4, 5).

I. Man Needs an Object of Worship.

A. One of the things that distinguishes men from animals is an inherent and intuitive sense of worship of some power higher than himself.
    1. All nations and peoples, no matter how primitive, have had their objects of worship, their gods, altars, sacrifices, and temples.
    2. History bears out the point affirmed in the Bible that man fell from the true worship of one God, Jehovah, into idolatry and polytheism (the worship of a plurality of gods) (Rom. 1:21-25; Eccl. 7:29).
    3. One of the dilemmas and frustrations of paganism and idolatry is that the gods men have created are obviously no higher in wisdom, strength, moral character, etc. than the men who created them. Hence, the gods of paganism are pictured as having human passions and catering to the lusts and desires of men. There were gods and goddesses of war, love, sex, fertility, etc. Read Jehovah's exposé of the vanity and futility of all these idols and false gods in Isaiah 44:8-21.
    4. In a prior lesson we established the fact that the God of heaven would have been to all mankind as He was to the people of Athens, "an unknown God" (emphasis mine, PJW – Acts 17:23), unless He had revealed Himself to man. But that revelation centered in and was manifested in His Son! What better way could God have used to show Himself as a Being worthy of man's worship and demonstrate His holiness, His power, His wisdom, His moral excellence, than to give to the world in the life of Jesus a living demonstration of His nature?
B. Jesus is Immanuel (God with us) (Matt. 1:23; Col. 2:9).
    1. John 1:1-4, 14, 18.
        a. Note: This One who is called "The Word" was with God in the beginning (Gen. 1:26 – "Let us make man") and He "is God" (i.e., He possesses all of the attributes of God, the Father). He is the same One who "became flesh and dwelt among us" (v. 14). When we see Jesus we see God in the flesh (v. 18).
    2. Colossians 1:15; Hebrews 1:1-3; 1 Timothy 3:16; Philippians 2:5-9.
        a. All of these passages affirm the same great truth of the Incarnation – that a Being with all the qualities of God took upon Himself human flesh and lived a physical existence on this earth.
        b. All that God is – love, mercy, grace, goodness, holiness, power – everything that would cause us to love and respect and obey Him was vividly demonstrated in the life of Jesus.
        c. Jesus manifested to the world a God who is:
            (1) Personal – He is our Father, He loves us and is concerned about us. He grieves at our sins and provides us a way of escape and a better way of life.
            (2) Moral – He is perfect in holiness, giving man an ideal toward which he can strive. He has no partiality (Acts 10:34, 35). He has none of the weaknesses and human propensities that characterized the heathen gods.

d. Man needed an object of worship who was higher in wisdom, power, and holiness than himself so that his worship would uplift and ennoble him rather than degrade him. Jesus answered the need perfectly by demonstrating in His life the qualities of God.

II. Man Needs a Sacrifice for Sin.

A. As universal as worship is the desire of man to be in favor with the Being (or beings) he worships.
1. All nations have had a concept of a fall from an original state of purity and innocence. All the sacrifices offered down through the centuries (animal or even human) have been an admission of man's sense of guilt and have shown his desire to regain the favor of the God (or gods) he has offended.
2. The Bible affirms this universality of sin (Rom. 3:23), and the alienation it produced (Isa. 59:1, 2) . God's law had been violated and His will trampled underfoot. Justice demanded that man must pay the penalty for such transgression. A government that does not punish wrongdoers is bound to fail; a law without penalties attached is useless (Heb. 2:2, 3).
3. Now, how could God uphold the validity of His law and meet the demands of Justice and yet at the same time extend mercy and grace to fallen man?

B. Once again Jesus answered the need! (John 1:29; 1 Pet. 2:24; Eph. 5:2; Rom. 4:25; 5:21; 1 Tim. 1:15).
1. The terribleness of sin was demonstrated in the tremendous price that was paid to cancel the debt of sin (John 3:16).
2. Because Jesus's act was voluntary, "He gave Himself for our sins" (Gal. 1:4), we see in it the greatest possible demonstration of sacrificial love. We admire and commend the actions of mothers and fathers who lay down their lives to save their children or of soldiers who give their lives to save a group of their comrades. How much more should we admire and appreciate the action of this sinless person who was willing to accept the death penalty for us and to accept the punishment that was due each one of us because of our transgressions of Divine Law (1 John 3:16).
3. In the Cross of Christ we see:
   a. Divine Justice Upheld – the penalty paid and the world taught that God's law cannot be broken with impunity.
   b. Divine Mercy Extended – God "gave His only begotten Son."
   c. Sacrificial Love Manifested – Jesus died "the just for the unjust"; He "bore our sins in His body."

III. Man Needs an Example of Manhood and Leadership.

A. From earliest childhood we are, consciously or unconsciously, imitators of others. Invariably we develop heroes whose lives we admire and after whom we strive to pattern ourselves. The influence of great men like Washington, Lincoln, Edison, Schweitzer, etc. is felt for generations after they live.
1. To be of true benefit to us the leader we choose to follow and imitate must possess greater wisdom, judgment, zeal, courage, and moral strength than we do. Only in this way can we be made better by following them.

NOTES

B. Jesus answers the need! He is leader, commander, and example!
   1. God promised such a leader (Isa. 55:4; Heb. 2:10).
   2. The essence of Christian living is to imitate, emulate, and follow His example (1 Pet. 2:21; Luke 9:23; Phil. 2:5; 1 John 2:6).
   3. Where could you find a more worthy example to follow? What leader ever demanded and received greater loyalty, devotion, and service? What leader has ever had the impact upon the world and influence for good that Jesus has? Who has ever been made worse by following His example?

IV. Man Needs a Friend.

A. Every normal person wants and needs the friendship of others, those whom he respects, admires, and has confidence in to whom he can turn for advice in times of decision, comfort in times of sorrow, or strength in times of weakness.
   1. But friendships are not always what they should be.
      a. There are "fair-weather" friends who desert us when we need them most.
      b. There are those who disappoint us, betray our confidence, and give us erroneous advice.
B. Jesus is a "friend that sticketh closer than a brother" (Prov. 18:24).
   1. To none can these words of Solomon be more applicable than to Jesus:
      a. Here is a Friend indeed!
      b. Here is a Friend who is completely unselfish, who loves us and sacrificed for us even though we did not earn or deserve that friendship (Rom. 5:6-8).
      c. Here is a Friend with amazing condescension, who gave up honor, glory, riches, etc., in order to prove His love for us (Phil. 2:4-8; 2 Cor. 8:9.)
      d. Here is a Friend who is constant, who is always there when we need Him, and who never changes (Heb. 13:8; Eph. 3:17-19).
      e. Here is a Friend with unlimited ability and resources. Worldly friends do not know our innermost thoughts and feelings. They may misjudge our motives or misinterpret our actions, and they may fail to bear, with sympathy and patience, our weaknesses. Not so with Jesus (Heb. 4:15, 16; Matt. 11:19).
      f. Here is a Friend who has proved Himself (John 15:13)! Truly we can sing with grace in our hearts "What a Friend we Have in Jesus!" But we must remember that true friendship cannot be one-sided; it must be reciprocated (John 14:15; 15:14; Prov. 18:24 (KJV) – "A man that hath friends must show himself friendly").

V. Man Needs a Hope.

A. From his earliest existence man has struggled for some hope:
   1. Something to sustain him in the trials and tribulations of life.
   2. Something to comfort him in sorrow.
   3. Something to give him courage as he faces serious illness and death.

NOTES

B. The false hopes entertained by man down through the years are simply expressions of the urgent and desperate need for a real hope:
   1. The Indian concept of a happy hunting ground.
   2. The Hindu concept of re-incarnation to a better existence.
   3. The still more vague and fanciful conceptions of a "Utopia," or "Shrangri-La," or "Fountain of Youth."
C. The dictionaries define "hopeless" as meaning "having no expectation," "forlorn," or "desperate."
   1. The only thing more pathetic than the person who entertains a false hope is the person who has lost all hope (Eph. 2:12).
D. But again, Christ supplies the answer – He is our Hope! (1 Tim. 1:1; Col. 1:27).
   1. Take away that Hope and the world would be shrouded in the blackest darkness (1 Cor. 15:19).
E. Upon what does a Christian hope rest?
   1. God's Promise (Titus 1:2).
      a. Men may make promises, excite our desire and expectation, and then go back on their word.
      b. But it is impossible that God could break a promise (Num. 23:19).
   2. God's Power (Mark 10:27).
      a. Men may make promises and sincerely desire to fulfil them but fail for lack of means.
      b. But whatever God promises He is able to fulfil (2 Tim. 1:12; Rom. 4:20, 21; Eph. 3:20).
   3. God's Record.
      a. Worldly persons' promises are measured by their past record at keeping their word (politicians, businessmen, etc.).
      b. Look at the record. Has God kept His promises in the past (Gen. 8:22; 9:15, 16; Deut. 18:15; Dan. 2:44)?
      c. We can put our trust in God's promises then because "He is faithful that promised" (Heb. 10:23).
   4. God's Oath (Heb. 6:13-20).
      a. If a man's word is considered more binding if he confirms it with a solemn oath, how much more the promise of God!
F. Hope is a combination of two essential elements – desire and expectation. The sinner is said to be "without hope" because:
   1. He cannot hope for heaven. He may desire to go to such a place but he has no basis for expecting to go there.
   2. He cannot even hope for hell. He may, if he believes the Bible at all, expect to go there, but surely does not desire to spend eternity in hell!
G. The hope entertained by Christians then is not some vague "pie-in-the-sky" day dream. It is based upon the word and promise, and even the oath of God, and it is centered in Christ. It is an anchor which we can tie our souls to in the storms and struggles of life (Heb. 6:19).

VI. Man Needs a Purpose in Life.

A. Ask any psychiatrist, sociologist, or psychologist what is wrong with modern man – why people are frustrated and unhappy, and why one out of eight people in this country will spend some time in a mental institution.

NOTES

1. Their answer may mention several factors but one will stand out – people are living meaningless lives, people have lost a real sense of purpose in their existence. "About a third of my cases are suffering from no clinically definable neurosis, but from the senselessness and emptiness of their lives" – Jung, Famous Psychiatrist.
    a. They set false goals and worship the false gods of money, fame, etc.
        (1) Those thousands who fail to achieve this false goal are disappointed, frustrated, and unhappy.
        (2) Those who achieve success find that it does not satisfy their innermost longings; there is always something lacking.
    b. Look about you in the world at the millions of people working, struggling, planning, grasping – FOR WHAT? How many have a worthwhile and meaningful goal or purpose in life?
B. This is exactly what the expression "lost" in the Bible conveys (Matt. 18:11).
    1. Dictionary definition – "having gone astray or lost the way, bewildered, perplexed, as a child lost in the woods."
    2. People by the millions have lost their bearings. They do not know where they are going or why they are going there. In fact, the Bible affirms that all men have lost the way (Rom. 3:11, 12, 23).
        a. Not only that, but they cannot find their own way (Jer. 10:23; Prov. 4:19; 13:15; 14:12).
        b. Neither can they rely upon the wisdom of others to show them the way (Matt. 15:14).
C. Again Jesus meets the need; He is the Way! (John 14:6).
    1. He is the only way of life, the only way to God (Jer. 32:39; Matt. 7:13, 14; Heb. 10:19, 20).
        a. He shows us the way to live.
        b. He shows us the way to die.
        c. His way brings us the greatest joy because it is based upon divine wisdom and it leads to home and to God.
        d. There is absolutely no other way, no other approach or access unto God (Eph. 2:18).
        e. That is why the best adjusted, the most serene and contended, and the happiest person you will ever know is the faithful Christian.
    2. Are you in that way (Gal. 3:27; 2 Cor. 5:17)?
        a. When Saul of Tarsus went out to persecute those of "the way," who did he persecute? Those in the church of Jesus Christ (Acts 22:4; 9:1; 8:3).

VII. Man Needs Freedom.

A. The history of man is a record of a long and ceaseless struggle to be free. (The children of Israel in Egypt, the pioneers in this country, the new African nations, the Blacks, etc.).
    1. The struggle for freedom from tyranny, slavery, disease, ignorance, and poverty still occupies much of man's attention and efforts.
    2. But if we should succeed in securing freedom from all political and social tyranny, there is still a form of bondage common to all mankind in which we would still be involved, the bondage of sin (John 8:34; Rom. 6:16, 17; 2 Pet. 2:19).

NOTES

B. Again Jesus supplies the answer, He is the Truth (John 14:6).
   1. Jesus is truly the Great Emancipator, the Deliverer of Man (John 8:36; Rom. 11:26; Gal. 1:3, 4; 1 Thess. 1:10).
   2. The medium Jesus has used to effect this deliverance is the Truth (John 8:31, 32; 17:17).
   3. That we value and love that Truth above every other consideration in life, that we believe and obey it, is absolutely essential to our salvation (Prov. 23:23; 1 Pet. 1:22; 2 Thess. 2:12).

VIII. Man Needs an Abundant Life.

A. Inherent within man is the desire for the "good life," the "abundant life," the "happy life." There has to be more to man's life than the mere existence of eating, sleeping, working, etc.
   1. Our constitution and similar documents throughout the world recognize as God-given and inalienable the rights of life, liberty, and the pursuit of happiness.
   2. Men have died to defend our rights to "pursue" happiness, great statesmen have written and debated upon this pursuit of happiness, but with all their wisdom they have failed to tell us where to find it!
   3. In this "land of the free and home of the brave" we see close to 200 million people running to and fro, pursuing, chasing happiness and the abundant life and very few ever finding it.
   4. The frustrations, disappointments, and disillusionments of this vain search for the better and happy life is written across the pages of human history.
      a. No person better personifies and illustrates that frantic and empty search than does Solomon as he outlines his search for happiness in the book of Ecclesiastes.
         (1) Like many, he thought "the good life" meant riches, but this failed to bring him happiness (Eccl. 5:10; Prov. 11:4, 28).
         (2) Like many, he thought "the good life" meant laying up worldly wisdom and knowledge and this too failed to satisfy his needs (Eccl. 1:13, 17, 18).
         (3) Like many he imagined that the "good life" was to satisfy fleshly desires, to live for pleasure, and to "eat, drink, and be merry," and this too left an empty void (Eccl. 2:1, 10, 17).
      b. The experience of Solomon has been, and is being, re-lived in the lives of countless millions. People are still trying the same worn out old paths to find the "good life," yet there is always that feeling of "vanity" and "striving after the wind," the feeling that there has to be something better, something more meaningful, and something more conducive to happiness. But what and where is it?

B. Again Jesus supplies the answer – He is the Life (John 14:6; 10:10; 20:21).
   1. Jesus's primary purpose in coming into the world was to bring Life (John 11:25; 5:40).
   2. Not only does Jesus offer the better, the fuller, the more abundant life here but, more than that, eternal life (1 John 5:11, 12).
      a. It is obvious that this gift of eternal life is located "In His Son" ... if you are in Christ, you have that life. If you are not "in Christ" you do not have it.
      b. The significance of scriptural baptism (an immersion in water for the remission of sins upon our confession of faith in Him) can be seen in that it puts us into Christ where that life is found (Gal. 3:27; Rom 6:4, 5).
   3. In that life, the "new life," the "abundant life," there is true and lasting happiness (Psa. 144:15; Jer. 9:23, 24; Eccl. 12:13).

IX. Man Needs Peace.

A. The struggle for peace is as old as man himself. All over the world prayers are offered, books are written, and governments meet in conference, in a compelling quest for peace.
   1. But it is not just world peace that man seeks and needs desperately, but more importantly still, peace with God and peace within himself.

2. The chaotic condition in our country and in the world is but an outward expression of the unrest, unhappiness, and emotional instability of millions of people.
3. One of the greatest causes of this general lack of peace of mind is a sense of guilt. Man knows that he cannot hope for peace with self until he is at peace with God (Col. 1:21; Eph. 4:18; Jas. 4:4).

B. Again, Christ meets the need – He is our Peace (Eph. 2:14).
1. Peace of mind is not something that you can get out of a bottle of tranquilizers, or in a book written by man, or on a psychiatrist's couch (while these may all have their place); it is a Divine legacy that Jesus left to His disciples (John 14:27).
    a. This peace can only come by faith (Rom. 5:1).
    b. This peace is found only in Christ (John 16:33; Phil. 4:7).
    c. This peace is enjoyed only in the body (or church) of Christ (Col. 3:15).

X. Man Needs Health.

A. The world is extremely health-conscious. Millions are spent yearly on health magazines, health foods, and health fads. Doctors are doing a thriving business and admit that a large percentage of those who visit them have nothing organically wrong with them. Physical culture classes, gymnasiums for body building, etc. are doing a booming business. Billions of dollars are spent each year in research and treatment to fight the enemies of health.
1. One of the greatest incongruities in all this emphasis on physical health is the tendency to ignore almost completely our spiritual health.
    a. Man is a dually natured creature having both body and soul (Matt. 10:28; 2 Cor. 4:16; 2 Cor. 5:1; Phil. 1:21-24).
    b. God's evaluation of the body is that of a tent, a temporary dwelling place (Job. 14:1; Psa. 90:10; Jas. 4:14).
    c. The Bible places the greater emphasis upon our spiritual health rather than our physical health (Matt. 4:4; Luke 12:19-23; Matt. 16:26).
2. Just a casual look at the world with the growing incidence of crime, hatred, violence, war, divorce, dope addiction, alcoholism, etc. should convince us that the world is truly sick (Isa. 1:5, 6).
    a. When all of man's remedies fail, people cry out with Jeremiah, "Is there no balm in Gilead. Is there no Physician there?" (Jer. 8:22).

B. Again, Jesus is the answer; He is the great physician (Mark 2:17).
1. He has all the qualifications:
    a. His knowledge is infinite! (Col. 2:3).
    b. His power is unlimited! (Matt. 28:18).
    c. His success is phenomenal. He has never failed in any case where complete trust and confidence were put in Him.
    d. His terms are amazing. "Without money and without price" (Isa. 55:1).

Conclusion:

Every need of man is freely and completely answered in Jesus. Without Him you rob yourself of all these blessings and more. Without Him you can do nothing (John 15:5). Without Him you cannot please God (Rom. 8:8).

Why You Need Baptism

You **BAPTISM**

Gal. 3:27	In Christ	2 Cor. 5:17; Eph. 1:3, 7; 2 Tim. 2:10; Rom. 8:1
Gal. 3:26-27	Child of God	1 John 3:1; Rom. 8:16-17
John 3:5	Kingdom of God	1 Cor. 15:24
Gal. 3:27	Way of Life	John 14:6; Matt. 7:13-13
1 Cor. 12:13	Church (Body)	Eph. 1:23; 2:16; 3:16, 21; 5:23
Rom. 6:4	Death (Blood)	Matt. 26:28; Heb. 9:22; Rev. 1:5-6; 1 John 1:7; 5:8
Matt. 28:19-20	Name	Luke 24:47; Acts 4:12; Col. 3:17; Phil. 2:9
1 Pet. 3:21	Saved	Mark 16:16
Acts 22:16	Sins Washed Away	

"There Is... One Baptism" (Eph. 4:4-5)

Subject	Mode	Element	Purpose
Infant?	Sprinkling, Pouring, or Immersion?	Holy Spirit?	Sign Already Saved?
Believer?		Water?	Remission of Sins?

Lesson 7

Why You Need Baptism

Introduction:

A. We have thus far established the following propositions:
   1. There is a God.
   2. God created man in His image.
   3. God revealed Himself and His will to man and that revelation is found in the Bible.
   4. The fundamental truth of that revelation is that Jesus Christ is the Son of God.
   5. God's authority in this dispensation is exercised in and through Christ and (by delegation of authority) through His chosen apostles and their recorded word which is all sufficient as a revelation (2 Tim. 3:16, 17).

B. What we read in the New Testament scriptures then concerning Baptism, or any other subject, is nothing less than the Word of God and is as compelling and binding as if He spoke directly and audibly to us (1 Thess. 2:13). What we think, what our parents taught us, what creed books or human wisdom dictate, or what we've always believed about the matter is to be set aside in favor of the question "What saith it?" – What? "the word of faith which we (apostles ... PJW) preach" (Rom. 10:8).

I. Attitudes toward Baptism in the Religious World.

A. To many people baptism is just a ceremony whereby a baby is given a name and a special blessing from God; to others baptism is simply "an outward sign of an inward grace" – something you go through to convince the world that you are already saved; to others baptism is simply a ceremony which puts one into some denominational church; and to still others, baptism is a "sacrament," the means by which "original sin" is taken away.

B. There are two general attitudes concerning the design and purpose of Baptism.
   1. Baptism is Essential.
      a. The Roman Catholic doctrine of "baptismal regeneration" makes baptism absolutely necessary since according to their writings "baptism is a sacrament which cleanses us from original sin" (*Visible Church*, by Sullivan, 39). The Catholic Church feels so strongly about the efficacy of just a few drops of water to cleanse from so called "original sin" (i.e., the guilt of sin inherited from Adam) that they even have nurses in Catholic hospitals baptize (?) infants born dead. The following quotation from "The Catholic Nurse and the Dying" by Bowdern, will give an idea of the ridiculous extremes they go to in administering this false doctrine:

         Human life, and therefore the soul, is present at the moment of conception. For this reason an embryo, even in early miscarriage, has an immortal soul. If the embryo can be recognized, take it in your fingers and dip it under the water and lift it out again while you pronounce the words of Baptism. In case you cannot recognize the embryo at all, pour water on the blood clot in the miscarriage; and pronounce the words of Baptism (Quoted in *American Freedom and Catholic Power*, by Paul Blanchard, 138).

      b. The New Testament position also makes baptism essential for the remission of our own past sins (not original or inherited sins). The proposition to be proved in this lesson is that water baptism for the penitent believer is essential to the remission of past sins.
   2. Baptism is Non-Essential. This is the general denominational attitude as expressed in their creed books.

       a. Methodist – "Wherefore that we are justified by faith only is a most wholesome doctrine and very full of comfort" (Article 9, *Discipline of Methodist Episcopal Church, South*, 1910). (It is obvious from this statement, and similar ones to follow, that if we are saved by faith only, baptism has no part in that salvation. Incidentally this statement stands in direct contradiction to Jas. 2:24.)
       b. Episcopal – Article 11 of *Episcopal Articles of Religion* is the same as the Methodist statement in Article 9.
       c. Church of the Nazarene – "That believers are to be sanctified wholly – through faith in the Lord Jesus Christ" (*Manual*, 1956, page 36).
       d. Baptist – "All you have to do is believe and He will save you" also, "justification, the pardon of sin, and the promise of eternal life – are solely through faith" (J. M. Pendleton, *Church Manual for Baptist Churches*, 48, emphasis mine, PJW).
"We hold that Baptism is not essential to salvation" (*Hiscox Manual for Baptist Churches,* 20).
       e. "Jehovah's Witnesses" – "repentance must precede baptism but sins are not washed away by baptism" (*Make Sure of All Things,* article on Baptism, 30).
       f. Presbyterian – "yet grace and salvation are not so inseparably annexed unto it (baptism), as that no person can be regenerated or saved without it."
   3. Obviously baptism cannot be at the same time "essential" and "non-essential." Let us turn then from the writings and authority of men to the Word of God for light on this important subject.

II. The Essentiality of Baptism Can Be Seen in What Scriptural Baptism Does for Us.

   A. Baptism stands between you and being "in Christ."
      1. Galatians 3:27.
        a. Whatever the phrase "in Christ" means, whatever blessings are to be found in that relationship, one thing is obvious … it is baptism that puts you INTO Christ, or into that relationship designated as "in Christ." Before you are baptized, you are not in Christ, after you are scripturally baptized you are "in Christ."
        b. It is not said of faith or repentance or confession that they put us Into Christ. They are said to be steps "UNTO" (in the direction of) salvation in Christ (Rom. 10:10; Acts 11:18). But baptism puts us "INTO" (from without to within) Christ.
      2. Why do we need to be In Christ? This is beyond question one of the most significant phrases in the New Testament. All of the provision that the grace and love of God have made for the happiness and eternal salvation of man has been centered in and summed up "in Christ" (Eph. 1:3, 7; 2 Cor. 5:17; 2 Tim. 2:10; Rom. 8:1; John 15:5; Rev. 14:13).
   B. Baptism stands between you and being a child of God.
      1. Galatians 3:26-27.
        a. Many quote v. 26 – "For ye are all sons of God, through faith, in Christ Jesus" – and leave off v. 27. However, the preposition "for" in the beginning of v. 27 shows that they are connected and that the means by which those who have faith in Christ become sons of God is by being baptized into Christ (John 1:12 shows that believing in Christ gives us the power or the right

to become children of God, it does not itself make us children of God.)
2. "But," some ask, "Is it not true that all humankind are children of God?" "Did He not create us all?"
   a. We need to distinguish between being a part of the human family and being a member of God's spiritual family. The Jews made the mistake of assuming that they were God's children when in reality they were children of the Devil (John 8:31, 40-44).
   b. What a wonderful thought it is to know that God is your spiritual Father! But only those who have obeyed the truth, who have been born again, who have been redeemed by the blood of Christ, have the right to "call on him as Father" (1 Pet. 1:17-24; 1 John 3:1).
   c. To be a child of God means that we have His love and care watching over us. It means that He will not withhold any good thing from us (Matt. 7:9-12). It means that we are heirs of God, joint heirs with Christ (Rom. 8:16, 17).

C. Baptism stands between you and being in the Kingdom of God.
   1. John 3:3-5.
      a. Notice that there are not two births, one of water and one of spirit, but rather one birth with both spirit and water factors involved (just as we have one physical birth in the natural realm with two factors, male and female, involved).
         (1) The Spirit's part – This is the planting of the seed (the word of God – Luke 8:11) into the spiritual heart of man. Of course, this is through the medium of gospel teachers (John 6:45). When we believe the message of the Spirit we are said to be "begotten" of the Spirit (Jas. 1:18).
         (2) The water's part – the only thing with which water is associated in the Christian religion is baptism.
      b. What Jesus had taught in figures of speech before His death, He taught the Apostles plainly after His resurrection. In Mark 16:15, 16 we find this teaching on the new birth set forth in plain and unmistakable terms.
         (1) "Go – Preach" … The seed of the Kingdom (the Gospel) has to be planted.
         (2) "He that believeth" … is begotten, the word finding lodgement and root in his heart.
         (3) "Shall be saved" … is born again (of water and the spirit) and has a new life in Christ.
   2. But what does it mean to be In the kingdom of God?
      a. It means that you will be in that group that is delivered up to God in the final day (1 Cor. 15:24).
      b. It means to be delivered from the power of darkness and to be translated into that realm where redemption and forgiveness of sins are found (Col. 1:13, 14).
      c. It means to be a subject of, and recipient of the blessings of Christ the King. It ought to be obvious to any thinking person that a person cannot be under the authority or rule of Christ unless he is in the kingdom over which He is King.

D. Baptism stands between you and being in the way of life.
   1. Galatians 3:27; John 14:6.

NOTES

            a. We have already seen that we are baptized "into Christ," but Christ is "the way," therefore, we are baptized into that way.
        2. Why is it so important for one to be in "the way"?
            a. There are only two ways of life that man can take, one leads to eternal life, the other to destruction (Matt. 7:13, 14).
                (1) The Broad Way.
                    (a) It is the popular way ("many" are taking it).
                    (b) Those taking it can be self deceived (Prov. 12:15; 16:25).
                    (c) It is a dark, and hard, and crooked way (Prov. 4:9; 13:15; Psa. 21:8).
                (2) The Narrow Way.
                    (a) It is the "good way" (Jer. 6:16); the "one way" (Jer. 32:39, 40); the "way of Holiness" (Isa. 35:8); the "new and living way" (Heb. 10:20).
                    (b) It is the only way to Heaven (John 14:6).
    E. Baptism stands between you and being in the church (or body) of Christ.
        1. 1 Corinthians 12:13.
            a. This is the only means by which people can enter the body (or church) of Christ. You cannot "join" it or be "voted" into it, but as those in the early church, you must enter by baptism (Acts 2:41, 47).
        2. Why is it so essential for one to be in the church or body?
            a. If you are not in the body, Christ is not your Head (Eph. 1:22, 23). You deny Him the right to regulate and control your life. You, like a hand severed from a physical body, cut yourself off from the life and sustenance in His body (v. 23 "fulness").
            b. If you are not in the body you are not reconciled to God (Eph. 2:16).
            c. If you are not in the body, you are not a "fellow-heir" or a "fellow-partaker of the promise in Christ Jesus" (Eph. 3:6). Neither are you in the realm where you can glorify God by your life (Eph. 3:21).
    F. Baptism stands between you and being in the death of Christ, or being a recipient of the benefits of His blood.
        1. Romans 6:3, 4.
            a. Whatever benefits the death of Christ or the blood of Christ can bring to us, it is obvious that it is scriptural baptism that puts us "into His death" (or into that realm where His blood can cleanse us).
        2. What are the benefits of His death or His blood?
            a. Without it, we have no remission of sins (Matt. 26:28; Heb. 9:22; Rev. 1:5, 6).
            b. Without it, we cannot be brought near to God (Eph. 2:13).
            c. Without it, we cannot be washed from our sins and made a part of God's Kingdom (Rev. 1:5, 6).
            d. If you are not in the body, you are not in that group that Jesus has promised to save (Eph. 5:23).

NOTES

3. In Romans 6 we can see the power of His blood in the change that took place when they were baptized.
    a. Before baptism they were:
        (1) Dead in sin, in bondage to sin (v. 6).
        (2) Servants of sin (v. 17).
        (3) Due the wages of sin – death (v. 23).
    b. After baptism they were:
        (1) Dead to sin (v. 2, 11).
        (2) Raised to walk a new life (v. 4).
        (3) Old man crucified, body of sin done away (v. 6).
        (4) Alive unto God in Christ (v. 11).
        (5) Made free from sin (v. 17).
        (6) Servants of righteousness (v. 18).
        (7) Had the promise of eternal life (vv. 22, 23).

G. Baptism stands between you and the name of Christ.
    1. Matthew 28:19, 20 (ASV).
        a. The essentiality of baptism can be seen in that it is the only command in the Bible coupled with the name of the Sacred Three (Father, Son, Holy Spirit).
        b. A person is not only baptized "in the name of" (by the authority of), but also "into the name of" (into a special relationship with) the Father, Son, and Holy Spirit.
    2. The significance of the name of Christ.
        a. It is connected to the remission of sins (Acts 10:43, NOTE: "through His name").
        b. It is connected with salvation (Acts 4:12).
        c. It is above every name (Phil. 2:9).
        d. In order to wear anyone's name in religion, two things must be true:
            (1) They must have been crucified for you.
            (2) You must have been baptized into their name (1 Cor. 1:12, 13).

H. Baptism stands between you and salvation.
    1. 1 Peter 3:21.
        a. All of the sophistry and human widom in the world cannot erase the plain fact stated by Peter that "baptism doth also now save us."
        b. Because the salvation of Noah was a figure, or type, of our salvation by baptism, some have concluded that the baptism is not literal. But that is not the point. Just as Noah and his family were delivered from the old degenerate world into a new life "by water," so we are delivered from the old life of sin into a new life of righteousness by baptism.
        c. Does this mean "water salvation"? If by that expression people mean that God used water as the instrument of our salvation, then we are saved by baptism, just as Noah and his family were saved by water. But if by that expression people mean salvation by water to the exclusion of faith, grace, obedience, etc., the answer would be "no." Besides water, Noah was saved by grace (Gen. 6:8), by faith (Heb. 11:7), by obedience (Heb. 11:7; Gen. 7:5).

NOTES

I. Baptism stands between you and having your sins washed away.
    1. Acts 22:16.
        a. Whatever the washing away of sins means, it is apparent that we must be baptized in order to receive it. Of course, it is the blood of Christ that has the power to wash away sins (Rev. 1:5, 6), but it is in baptism that we reach His death (Rom. 6:4).
            (1) Surely if our sins are forgiven at the moment of faith then there could be no relationship between baptism and the forgiveness of sin.
    2. Acts 2:38.
        a. "Sins washed away" and "remission of sins" are synonymous terms, and in both these passages baptism came before the blessing.
        b. Some have suggested that this baptism was "to show their sins were already remitted." But consider the context. These people had been cut to the heart, convicted by preaching that accused them of murdering the Son of God. Their logical question was, "What shall we do?" – for what? To show they were already saved? This would be ridiculous! No, they were asking what they should do to have their sins forgiven and the answer was "repent and be baptized for the remission of sins."
J. Now the sum of what we have said in this section is simply this: if being in Christ is essential, if being a child of God is essential, if being in the kingdom of God is essential, if walking in the narrow way is essential, if being in the church or body of Christ is essential, if the blood and name of Christ are essential to our salvation, then baptism is essential since it is baptism that puts us into all these relationships and blessings.

III. Essentiality of Baptism Seen Also in the Cases of New Testament Conversion.

A. Acts 2:36-41.
B. Acts 8:5, 12. 13.
C. Acts 8:35-39.
D. Acts 9:1-19; 22:6-16.
E. Acts 10.
F. Acts 16:13-14.
G. Acts 16:26-34.
H. Acts 18:8.
I. Several pertinent facts emerge as we examine these cases:
    1. Every one of them follows the pattern set forth in the Great Commission (Matt. 28:18-20; Mark 16:15-16). The gospel was preached, people believed it, and were baptized.
    2. In no instance was any person ever called a "Christian," ever said to be "saved," or ever said to be a member of the church until after he had been baptized.
    3. If under the direction of inspired apostles and Spirit-guided preachers, baptism was preached as essential and was administered the "same hour of the night," we should respect and follow that pattern.

IV. What Constitutes Scriptural Baptism?

A. The Denominational view.
1. Webster and other modern dictionaries often define the word "baptism" so as to include either "sprinkling, pouring, or immersion."
   a. Of course dictionaries define a word according to its modern usage and since these three forms are commonly practiced as "baptism" today, these are proper modern definitions.
   b. There is a rule of interpretation that is applicable here. It says "the proper definition of a term substituted for it will always make as good sense as the term itself." Now if "sprinkle" or "pour" are proper definitions of the Greek word *bapto* or *baptidzo* these words could be substituted in any passage where the word "baptism" or "baptize" is used. Try the word "sprinkle" for example in such contexts as (emphasis mine, PJW):
      (1) John 3:23 – "And John also was sprinkling in Aenon near to Salim because there was much water there." Does that make sense?
      (2) Acts 8:38 – "And he commanded the chariot to stand still: and they both went down into the water, both Philip and the Eunuch; and he *sprinkled* him." Does that fit the sense of the context?
      (3) Colossians 2:12 – "Having been buried with him in *sprinkling*, wherein ye were also raised with him through faith in the working of God... ." Are people "buried" and "raised" in sprinkling?
      (4) Now if you try "immerse" in the passages just read, it would fit the context in every case.
2. The fact is that "baptism" is not strictly an English word, but an Anglicized Greek word. The dilemma of sectarian and denominational scholars in translating the Greek words *bapto* or *baptidzo* into English is obvious:
   a. If they translated it "immerse," that would rule out "sprinkle" or "pour" (which were already in common use when the translations were made).
   b. If they translated it "sprinkle" or "pour" that would rule out "immersion" (which had been in common use since the first century).
   c. Furthermore, if they used the Anglicized word "baptize" to include all three ideas consistency would demand that in order to meet the demands of the word "baptize," they would have to "immerse, sprinkle, and pour" ... all three!
3. The best way to find the meaning of a Greek word is to go to a Greek-English lexicon. This is the language in which the New Testament was written and hence such a lexicon would give the true meaning, rather than the "modern usage." The testimony of 65 or 70 Lexicons is overwhelming as to the action of baptism as will be seen from the following samples:
   a. Bagster – "to dip; to immerse."
   b. Bloomfield – "to immerse, to sink."
   c. Constantine – "immerse, plunge, dip, bathe."
   d. Donnegan – "to immerse ... to submerge, to sink."
   e. Green – "to dip; immerse."

    f. Greenfield – "immerse, immerge, submerge, sink."
    g. Grimm – "dip ... immerge, submerge."
    h. Liddell and Scott – "to dip in, or underneath water."
    i. Parkhurst – "to dip, immerse, or plunge in water."
    j. Robinson – "to immerse, to sink."
    k. Thayer – "to dip ... to immerse, submerge."
    l. Schoettgen – "to plunge, to immerse, to plunge in water."
  4. In spite of this evidence, many denominations practice sprinkling or pouring and some give the candidate a choice of all three.
    a. To add to the confusion, some churches still recognize Holy Spirit baptism or even baptism in fire as needful and desirable today.
    b. But bear in mind, in Ephesians 4:4-5, Paul said "there is ... one baptism." From the confusion of sectarian baptisms, we must distinguish always the "one baptism" ... the one ordained by Christ in the Great Commission, the one that can save us from past sins and put us into Christ.
B. The subject of the "one baptism."
  1. That God intended baptism to be administered only to a believer in Christ is evident from the following:
    a. Matthew 28:19, 20 – Teaching, believing, before baptism.
    b. Mark 16:15, 16 – Preaching, believing, before baptism.
    c. John 6:44, 45 – Hearing, learning before coming to Christ.
    d. Matthew 13:15 – Conversion predicated upon hearing with our ears and understanding in our heart.
    e. Acts 8:36, 37 – Note condition "if thou believest with all thy heart, thou mayest."
    f. Acts 18:8.
  2. These conditions would positively exclude infants who are not old enough to comprehend and believe the gospel, mentally incompetents who are not able to comprehend and believe the gospel, and all unbelievers who will not believe the gospel.
C. The mode of the "one baptism."
  1. Actually the expression "modes of baptism" is a misnomer, a contradiction of terms. Since the word "baptism" (*baptidzo*) describes a definite action (immersing, dipping, plunging, or submerging), sprinkling could not be a mode (or method) of doing it as this is another action altogether. It would be like saying "talking" is a "mode of transportation." The only mode or method that is acceptable to God is that which he word itself requires.
    a. Romans 6:4; Colossians 2:12 – Baptism is a "burial."
    b. Romans 6:5 – Baptism is a "planting."
    c. Acts 8:36-38 – Baptism necessitates going down into the water and coming up out of the water.
    d. Romans 6:4, 5; Colossians 2:12 – Baptism involves a resurrection, a being raised from the water.

            e. John 3:5 – Baptism involves a birth, a coming forth from, the water.
            f. Only total immersion in water can accomplish these requirements.
    D. The element of the "one baptism."
        1. That water, rather than the Holy Spirit, is the element of this "one baptism" is seen from the following:
            a. Romans 6:4, 5 – We are immersed into this element and raised from it leaving it behind. If this was the Holy Spirit, we wouldn't have it anymore.
            b. Mark 16:15, 16 – The apostles were charged with baptizing people as were other preachers (Acts 8). We know this could not be Holy Spirit baptism because only Jesus could administer this baptism (John 1:33, 34; Matt. 3:11).
            c. Acts 8:36-38; 10:47; Ephesians 5:26; Hebrews 10:22; 1 Peter 3:20, 21. Water is specifically mentioned as the element of New Testament baptism.
        2. Holy Spirit baptism, which was a promise, not a command to be obeyed, and which was never promised to mankind in general, or even all believers, served its purposes in the guidance and inspiration of the apostles (John 14:26; 16:13; Acts 1:2-5; 2:1-4) but water baptism as a command for all believers to obey still remains.
    E. The purpose of the "one baptism."
        1. As we have seen in all of the passages studied, baptism was not just a sign to show one is already saved, or to name a baby, or to join a church – baptism is for the remission of sins (Acts 2:38); the washing away of sins (Acts 22:16); the salvation from past sins (Mark 16:16).
    F. Having eliminated the unscriptural elements then we see that in order for us to experience the "one baptism" – a penitent believer must be immersed, in water, for the remission of sins. Anything less than that, anything other than that, no matter how well intended or sincerely engaged in, is not scriptural baptism.

V. **The Conclusion of the Matter.**

    A. After all the arguments are made, and all the theological smokescreens are laid down, and all the debates are held, the question of baptism still resolves itself down to this:
        1. Jesus, who died for you, asked you to do it (Mark 16:16).
        2. If you love Him, you will do it (John 14:15; Luke 6:46).
        3. If you want to please God, you will do it His way (Heb. 11:6; Rom. 10:17).

NOTES

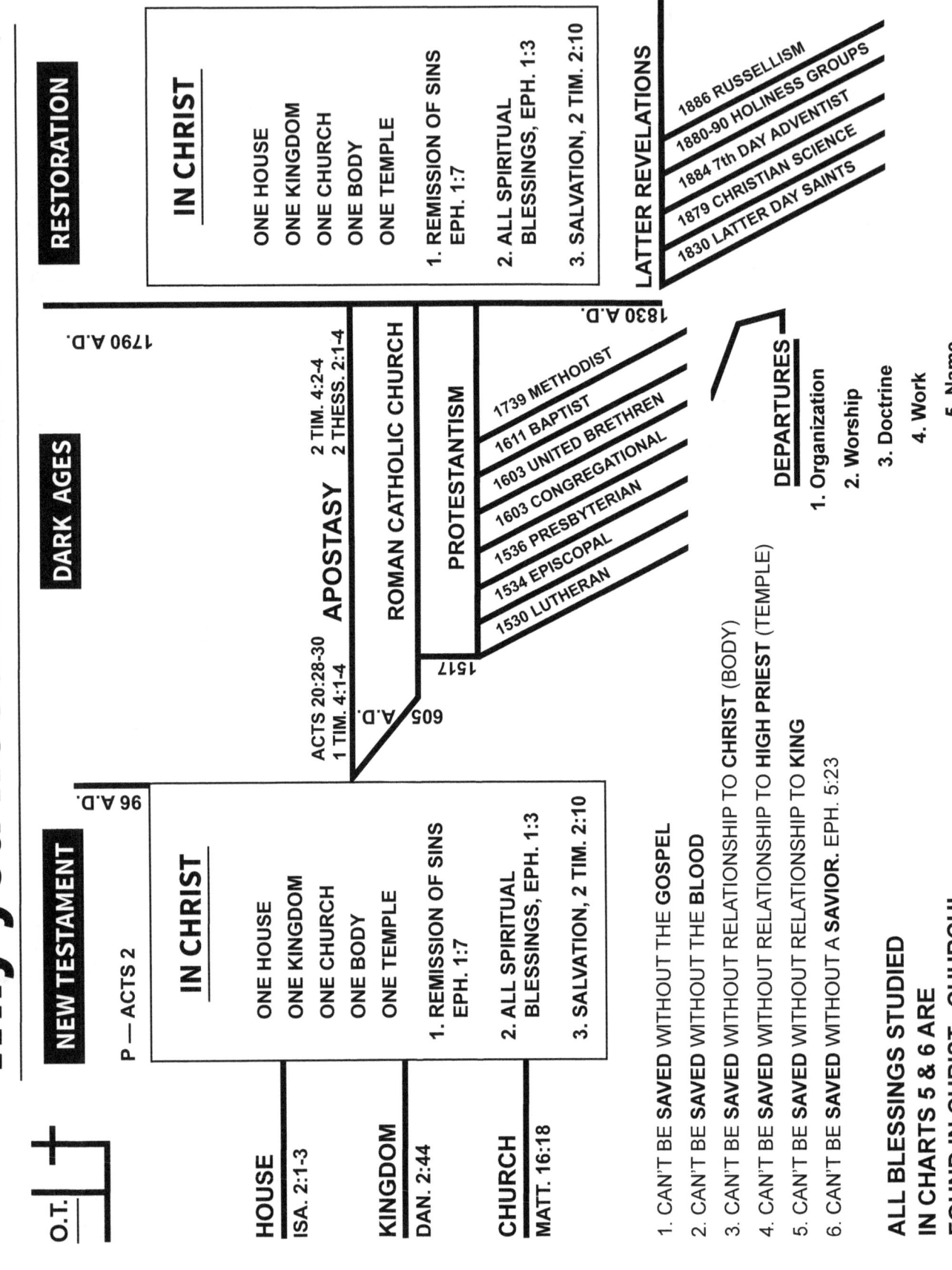

Lesson 8

Why You Need the Church

Introduction:
A. Review previous lessons.
   1. Special emphasis upon the last two lessons:
      a. We have found that all of God's plans and purposes centered in Jesus Christ; that all the provision God made for our spiritual welfare and salvation are to be found "in Him"; that we are truly "made complete" in Him (Col. 2:10); that He satisfies all of our spiritual needs.
      b. As Jesus is the savior in whom all these blessings become a reality to man, we have found also that scriptural baptism is the doorway into all these blessings as it puts us into Christ (Gal. 3:27), into His death (Rom. 6:4), into His name (Matt. 28:19, 20), into His body (1 Cor. 12:13), and into His Kingdom (John 3:5).
      c. In this lesson we want to emphasize that the church is the realm, or spiritual institution, in which these blessings from God through Christ are to be enjoyed and exercised.
      d. We want to divide our study of the church into the following categories:
         (1) The singularity or oneness of the church.
         (2) The chronology or history of the church.
         (3) The essentiality of the church.

I. The Singularity of the Church

   A. The problem of denominationalism.
      1. The picture of the religion of Jesus Christ that many millions of people are confronted with is one of confusion and division. There are more than 250 religious denominations wearing different names, teaching differing and even contradictory doctrines, having different forms of worship, and presenting different plans by which men might be saved. Yet they all claim to recognize the same God and Father, the same Lord Jesus Christ, and profess to follow the same Bible.
         a. To even a casual observer such a system is confusing. How many thousands have felt a need for Christ and His teaching in their lives and yet have taken one look at the divided and unsettled picture presented by denominationalism and have said, "If that is Christianity, I don't want it!"
         b. It is obviously a wasteful and extravagant system calling for the expenditure of billions of dollars yearly to oil denominational machinery, to build and maintain denominational institutions (colleges, benevolent and missionary societies, printing houses, etc.), and to promote sectarian loyalty. The efficiency and financial savings that would result if all professing Christians were members of one church, wearing one name, promoting one system of teaching is apparent to any thinking person.
         c. But besides being confusing and wasteful, the whole system is divisive. To promote denominationalism is to condone, encourage, and even foster division among those who claim to be the children of God. Some find themselves in the ludicrous position of acknowledging that people in other denominations than theirs are "Christians" and have the hope of heaven and yet they refuse to fellowship them in the Lord's Supper because of sectarian barriers.
         d. Denominationalism is a system self-condemned. The leaders of the religious world are all agreed that the system of denominationalism is indefensible. In the Second World Conference on Faith and Order of the World Council of Churches held in Edinburgh, Scotland, in 1937, the following resolution was adopted: "We humbly acknowledge that

our divisions are contrary to the will of Christ, and we pray God in His mercy to shorten the days of our separation and to guide us by His spirit into fullness of unity – we know that our witness is weakened by our divisions" (emphasis mine, PJW) (*Christian Forum*, Feb. 1, 1951). The irony of the whole thing is that while the leaders condemn division and have councils on unity, they are unwilling to lay aside the denominational creeds, names, organizations, etc., that create the division and return to God's plan. On a temporary basis they will set aside these sectarian names and creeds in order to have a "union meeting" or "campaign for Christ" in a given community. They grant that this will give them greater strength, more efficiency, and a stronger appeal during this soul-saving campaign but they fail to see the obvious fact that the same thing would be doubly effective on a long-term or permanent basis.

B. The Bible teaching on the singularity of the church.
   1. In the Old Testament.
      a. While it is true that the church is a New Testament institution, every prophecy concerning the church, every type or shadow pre-figuring the Church, in the Old Testament emphasizes the oneness of the Lord's church.
         (1) The Tabernacle or Temple: That these were a picture of the church to come is obvious from many passages (Zech. 6:12, 13; Amos 9:11, 12; Acts 15:14-19; Mal. 3:1; Heb. 8:2; 9:1-9, 11, 23; Eph. 2:19-22).
             (a) But there was only one tabernacle, only one temple, only one place where God's name was recorded and where His glory dwelt (Exod. 40:34-38; Deut. 12:5, 11; 1 Kings 8:10-13, 29).
             (b) When men built a counterfeit temple God would not recognize it (1 Kings 12:26-33).
         (2) The House of God: Another designation given to God's dwelling place on earth and used to prophetically picture the church Christ would build (1 Chron. 29:2; 2 Chron. 23:5; John 2:16; Isa. 2:2; Zech. 1:16; 1 Tim. 3:15).
             (a) But here again, God has only one house! It is always "The House of God," never in the plural!
         (3) The Flock (or Fold) of God: Another figure used to represent God's people in the Old Testament and to foreshadow the church of the New Testament is that of a flock (Jer. 13:17; 23:2; Acts 20:28, 29; 1 Pet. 5:2-4). But there is only one flock (John 10:14-16). NOTE: There are no more flocks than there are shepherds!
         (4) The Way: Another expression that denoted the people of God walking according to, and under, His rule in the Old Testament was "the way" (Pss. 1:6; 18:30; 25:9; 77:13; Prov. 10:29; Jer. 6:16). This term is also used prophetically and actually of the church [Isa. 35:8; Jer. 32:38-39; Acts 9:1, 2 (cf. 8:3); 19:8, 9, 23). But again, there is only one way (Jer. 32:39; Matt. 7:13, 14; John 14:6].
         (5) The Holy Nation, or Purchased Possession: Of all the nations of the world, God separated Israel to be His peculiar (or purchased) possession. They were a Holy nation because of their identity with Him (Exod. 19:5-6; Deut. 4:31-34; Ezek. 37:22; Psa. 135:4). But there was only one nation that wore God's name, that were His chosen people,

that had a covenant with Him. This "shadow" or "type" is fulfilled in the church today. It is the "nation born at once" (Isa. 66:8); it is the "strong nation" over which the Lord would reign (Mic. 4:1-7); it is the "chosen generation, a royal priesthood, a holy nation, a peculiar people" (1 Pet. 2:9); it is the "one nation" prophesied of in Ezekiel 37:22.
2. In the New Testament.
   a. Every figure used to identify the church in the New Testament (besides the five we have already studied from Old Testament prophecy) emphasizes its singularity.
      (1) Kingdom: The terms "church" and "kingdom of God" or "kingdom of Heaven" are used interchangeably in the New Testament. (Matt. 16:18, 19; Heb. 12:23, 28; Col. 1:13, 18). But the term "kingdom" is always used in the singular when pertaining to God's plan. Christ is the King, over the kingdom.
      (2) Body: That the terms "church" and "body" are likewise used synonymously is evident from these passages (Col. 1:18, 24; Eph. 1:22, 23).
         (a) Study carefully Ephesians 4:4, 5.
            (i) "There is one body." If the body is the church, then there is only one church (Eph. 2:16; 1 Cor. 12:12, 13, 20). The figure itself would demand one head (Christ), over one body (the church). Denominationalism puts Christ in the ludicrous position of being one head hundreds of bodies. This is a monstrosity!
            (ii) What if a person believes in two Gods, can he be a Christian? No, because the passage says "one God."
            (iii) What if a person believes in two Lords, can he be a Christian? No, because the passage says "one Lord."
            (iv) Yet how can people be Christians who believe in hundreds of churches (or bodies) when the passage says "one Body"? How can they believe in many differing "faiths," when the passage says "one faith"?
      (3) Bride: The church of the Lord is likewise portrayed as being married to Christ (John 3:28, 29; 2 Cor. 11:2; Rom. 7:4).
         (a) Study carefully Ephesians 5:23.
            (i) Note the definite article "the." Just as "the" (one) husband is "the" (one) head of "the" (one) wife, so Christ is "the" (one) head of "the" (one) church.
            (ii) One man married to one woman is God's plan. One man cannot be married to thousands of women, neither can Christ be the husband of thousands of wives (or churches). Denominationalism would make a spiritual polygamist out of Jesus!
      (4) Church: The term "church" is always used in the singular whenever it is talking of the church universal. Matthew 16:18, "... Upon this rock I will build my church (singular) and the gates of hell shall not prevail against it (not them)" (emphasis and parenthetical statements mine, PJW).
         (a) NOTE: In passages such as Romans 16:16, "The churches of Christ salute you" or Revelation 1:4, "The seven Churches of Asia," the reference is to local

NOTES

congregations, not to denominations of differing faith and order.
- C. Appeals for maintaining this oneness or unity and warnings against division.
  1. The appeal for unity (Psa. 133:1; Rom. 15:5, 6; Acts 4:32; 1 Cor. 1:10: Phil. 3:16).
     a. Is that the picture presented by denominationalism? Do they all with "one mind and one voice" glorify Sod? Do they all "speak the same things" and "walk by the same rule"? Are they all of "one heart and one soul"?
     b. Ephesians 4:3-5. This is something that Christians are to "endeavor" or "give diligence" to keep. Yet there is no possible way to reconcile the picture of denominationalism to God's platform for unity.
     c. John 17:20, 21. In the dark hours before His betrayal, this subject of the oneness of His followers was paramount in Jesus's thoughts and prayers. No way can possibly be found to reconcile the division and confusion of denominationalism to this prayer. Not even the conglomeration or federation of all sectarian churches into some ecumenical body would suffice as the unity Christ prayed for "that they all may be one, even as Thou art in Me, and I in Thee."
  2. Warnings against division (Rom. 16:17; Gal. 5:19-21).
     a. Notice that in Galatians 5 (ASV) "factions, divisions, parties" are classified in the same category as idolatry, fornication, drunkenness, revellings, etc.
- D. To sum up this section then, God planned and purposed one kingdom, one flock, one way, one house, one temple, or one church. Jesus built but one church. All Christians in the first century were members of that one church. The whole system of denominationalism and religious division is not only a modern innovation but is condemned as contrary to God's plan for unity.

II. The Chronology or History of the Church.

- A. The Church in God's eternal plan and purpose.
  1. Ephesians 3:8-10.
     a. Just as the sacrifice of Jesus for our sins was planned and purposed from the very foundation of the world (1 Pet. 1:19, 20; Rev. 13:8), so the church or kingdom as the realm in which that salvation might be enjoyed was planned from the beginning of time.
- B. The church in the prophecies of the Old Testament.
  1. As the house of God to be established in Jerusalem in the last days (Isa. 2:2, 3; Zech. 1:16).
  2. As the temple to be built by Christ (Zech. 6:12, 13; Amos 9:11, 12; Mal. 3:1).
  3. As the kingdom over which Christ would reign (Isa. 9:6, 7; Dan. 2:44; 7:13, 14).
  4. As Zion, the refuge of God's people (Isa. 24:23; 33:20-24; 46:13).
  5. For approximately 4,000 years then the spiritual institution referred to by the above mentioned figures existed only in Divine purpose, promise, and prophecy. The place of its establishment was set at Jerusalem, the time "in the last days" or "in the days of these kings (the Caesars), and the nature of it as a universal kingdom "all nations shall flow unto it."
- C. The church in the period of preparation during the lives of John the Baptist and Jesus.

1. When the time drew near for the fulfillment of all of these prophecies, there was a period of preparatory work, during which time the kingdom (or church) was announced to be "at hand" or "close by," or imminent (Matt. 3:1, 2; Mark 1:14, 15).
2. To see how immediate the prospect of the coming church or kingdom was, consider the following:
    a. It was to be in the lifetime of disciples living then (Mark 9:1).
    b. It was to be when the apostles received the outpouring of the Holy Spirit and its accompanying power (Mark 9:1; Acts 1:8), which event was "not many days hence" in Acts 1:4, 5.

D. The church in its actual establishment.
    1. On the Day of Pentecost, fifty days after the resurrection of Christ, as recorded in Acts 2 we find the culmination and fruition of more than 4,000 years of planning and prophecy.
        a. From Genesis 1 to Acts 2 there are hundreds of references to this spiritual institution, all pointing forward to a coming event.
        b. From Acts 2 on every reference to this spiritual institution is to an institution in actual existence.
            (1) The church was in existence (Acts 2:47; 8:2; 14:23).
            (2) The house of God was in existence (1 Tim. 3:15; Heb. 3:6).
            (3) The temple was in existence (Eph. 2:21, 22; 1 Cor. 3:16).
            (4) The kingdom was in existence (Col. 1:13; Heb. 12:28; Rev. 1:9; Matt. 26:29; 1 Cor. 11:23-28).
            (5) Spiritual Zion was in existence (Heb. 12:22-25).
            (6) The holy nation was in existence (1 Pet. 2:9).

E. The Church in perpetuity or the history of the Church since Pentecost.
    1. Bear in mind that the church or kingdom of God, once established was to continue until the end of the world and the second coming of Christ.
        a. Daniel 2:44; Isaiah 9:6, 7.
        b. Hebrews 12:28.
        c. The seed that produces the kingdom is the Word of God (Luke 8:11). Jesus said that this seed is indestructible (Matt. 24:35; 1 Pet. 1:23-25). Therefore the kingdom can never be destroyed and will be here when Christ comes to deliver it back to God (1 Cor. 15:24).
    2. Warnings of an apostasy.
        a. While the Apostles were still alive and the church was led by inspired men, it remained true to the pattern God had given. However, there were a number of warnings given about an apostasy, a falling away from the truth.
            (1) 2 Thessalonians 2:2-11.
            (2) 1 Timothy 4:1-4.
            (3) 2 Timothy 4:2-4.
            (4) Acts 20:28-30.
            (5) Summary of these passages:

NOTES

(a) An apostasy, a departure from the truth was sure to come.
(b) It would be characterized by the following:
  (i) Some would despise sound doctrine and turn to the fables of men.
  (ii) A group would arise who would forbid marriage and command abstinence from meats.
  (iii) From within this group would one arise setting himself forth as God, actually claiming titles and prerogatives that belong only to God.
  (iv) This apostasy would begin within the organization of the church – "from among your own selves."
(6) We identify this apostasy with the Roman Catholic Church.
  (a) Many have been taught that the Roman Catholic Church was the first church. This is not true. The church Jesus established through His Apostles was in existence 600 years before Catholicism as we know it developed.
  (b) Certainly Catholicism has many of the marks that were to characterize this apostasy.
    (i) It forbids marriage of priests and nuns.
    (ii) It commands abstinence from meats on fast days.
    (iii) The Pope of Rome actually occupies (in the mind of true Catholics) the position of God on earth. The official Catholic almanac makes this statement concerning the Pope: "the Pope is of so great dignity and so exalted that he is not a mere man, but as it were God, and the Vicar of Christ. He is also the Divine Monarch, the Supreme Emperor, and the King of Kings."
      (A) No man on earth has the right to such titles.
    (iv) Much of its tradition and doctrine is based on "fables" rather than the doctrine of Christ.
(7) How this Apostasy developed.
  (a) The pattern of church organization in the New Testament calls for:
    (i) A plurality of elders (bishops) in every local congregation (Phil. 1:1; Acts 14: 23; 20:17, 28; Titus 1:5, 7).
    (ii) Each local congregation is independent and autonomous.
  (b) 100 to 200 years after death of the Apostles.
    (i) Within an eldership, one man would become known as the ruling elder or presiding elder and gradually the term "bishop" was used to distinguish these ruling elders from the other elders (a distinction the Bible knows nothing of).
    (ii) Within a city of four or five congregations, one of these "bishops" would come to dominate all the others and finally became known as the City Bishop or "Patriarch" with authority over all the congregations in the diocese.
    (iii) These Patriarchs or City Bishops began to meet in councils (likewise unknown in New Testament times). In these councils there was a struggle for authority narrowing itself down to a fight between the Patriarchs of these five major cities: Jerusalem, Antioch, Constantinople, Alexandria, and Rome. This battle

for supreme authority finally narrowed down to the Bishop of Rome and the Bishop of Constantinople.
- (iv) In the Council of Chalcedon in A.D. 451, the Bishop of Constantinople tried to have himself appointed the "universal Bishop" or the head of the church on earth. He was opposed by Gregory, the Bishop of Rome (who has since been sainted by the Catholic Church). Gregory said that to assume the title of Universal Bishop or to seek to be the head of the church on earth was "the spirit of the Anti-Christ."
- (v) However, it was not very long after Gregory's death (A.D. 606) that Boniface III, then Bishop of Rome, succeeded in having himself declared the "universal Bishop" or Pope or head of the church on earth.

(c) During this period when the organization of the church was being corrupted there were likewise many corruptions in the worship and doctrine. (We have seen in previous lessons the completeness and sufficiency of the New Testament revelation and warnings against adding to or taking from the teaching of the Apostles.) The following things were added by the authority of man:
- (i) The use of Holy Water.
- (ii) Penance.
- (iii) Relics (pieces of the cross, bones of St. Peter, etc.).
- (iv) Burning of candles.
- (v) Burning of incense.
- (vi) Infant Baptism.
- (vii) Images.
- (viii) Counting of beads in prayer.
- (ix) Purgatory.
- (x) Celibacy of the Priesthood.
- (xi) Withholding the cup from the laity.
- (xii) Instrumental Music.
    - (A) Actually there are none of the things that distinguish the Roman Catholic Church that can be found in the Bible. Such things as a Pope, Cardinals, Archbishops, Nuns, etc., are unknown to the Scriptures.

(d) During this period (and for the next 1,000 years) Roman Catholicism reigned supreme over the religious world.
- (i) It is called the Dark Ages because the light of God's truth was practically covered up. The priests were the only ones who had access to the Bible and they interpreted it in the light of the teaching of the Church.
- (ii) Any opposition from so called "heretical" sects was stamped out by physical opposition. The Catholic Church administered capital punishment against those who did not bow to her authority.
- (iii) Any church history, including the *Catholic Encyclopedia,* will tell of the violence, the immorality of the Popes, the ridiculous superstitions and fables,

NOTES

etc., that characterized the apostate Church at this time.
3. The fundamental issue in all this is the matter of authority.
   a. We have already seen that all authority rests with Christ (Matt. 28:18).
   b. He entrusted this authority to His apostles (Matt. 16:18; 18:18).
   c. Their writings constitute the only and final authority in religious matters today (Gal. 1:8; 1 Cor. 4:6).
   d. The Roman Catholic Church on the other hand recognizes three sources of authority.
      (1) The Bible is recognized as inspired (with the qualification that it must be interpreted by the church).
      (2) The Pope when he speaks *ex cathedra* on matters of doctrine or morals is recognized as infallible.
      (3) Traditions of the church are likewise considered infallible.
         (a) Written traditions – the writings of the so-called "Church Fathers," men who lived and wrote in the early years of this apostasy.
         (b) Oral traditions – stories and fables handed down for generations by word of mouth are finally accepted as doctrine. (For example, the assumption of Mary, which was an oral tradition for centuries, and was made a dogma, recently.)
      (4) Actually, in practice, the Roman Catholic Church recognizes tradition above the word of God (as revealed in the New Testament). An example of this its seen in reference to the qualifications of a Bishop.
         (a) God in the Bible (1 Tim. 3:2) "The Bishop MUST be … the husband of one wife."
         (b) The Pope – a bishop cannot be married.
         (c) It is obvious whose word is respected as final in the Catholic Church.
4. The Protestant Reformation – 1517 to 1800 – The origin of denominationalism.
   a. Martin Luther, a Catholic monk and teacher in a Catholic University, nailed to the Church door at Wittenberg, Germany, 95 theses (or propositions for debate) objecting to the practices of the Catholic Church. This constituted the first major break with Catholicism. He was followed by men like Calvin, Zwingli, and others in a general defection from the yoke of Rome.
   b. There are several fundamental considerations that we need to keep in mind concerning this period:
      (1) This was a reformation movement, it was an attempt to reform an apostate organization.
      (2) Had these reforms been accepted, these men would have remained Roman Catholics.
      (3) When these reforms were rejected and these men were excommunicated, they started their own churches, something they had no authority from God to do. (The only one given authority to build a church was Christ – Matt. 16:18).
      (4) They naturally carried into these man-made churches many of the corruptions of Roman Catholicism.
         (a) While they left out such things as the Mass, the Pope, indulgences, etc., they brought over into these denominations such practices as infant baptism,

sprinkling, a clergy-laity distinction, instrumental music, etc.
- (5) They wrote human creeds to regulate and govern these churches that once again bound men to human authority and tradition in religion just as they had during the Dark Ages.
- c. From Luther's break with Rome in 1517, there has been a steady stream of human religious denominations:
  - (1) 1530 – The Lutheran Church established in Augsburg, Germany.
  - (2) 1534 – The Church of England was created by Henry VIII's break with the Pope. From this came the Episcopal Church.
  - (3) 1535 and 1536 – The Presbyterian Church was established by John Calvin in Switzerland and John Knox in Scotland.
  - (4) 1607 to 1611 – The Baptist Church was established by John Smythe in England.
  - (5) 1608 – The Congregational Church grew out of the Church of England.
  - (6) 1609 – The United Brethren grew out of a merger attempt between the Congregational and Presbyterian Churches.
  - (7) 1729 – The Methodist Church was established in England by John and Charles Wesley.
  - (8) 1844 – The Seventh Day Adventist Church in New England by Ellen G. White.
  - (9) 1830 – The Mormons (Church of Jesus Christ of the Latter Day Saints) in New England by Joseph Smith.
  - (10) 1878 to 1890 – The Christian Science (or Church of Christ, Scientist) in Boston by Mary Baker Eddy.
  - (11) Since then the list has continued with the Holiness Church, The Pentecostal, the Nazarene, Four Square, Mennonite, etc.
- d. At this point it is well to stress:
  - (1) That the church of Christ, the one body found in the Bible had been in existence for more than 1500 years before these human churches were built.
  - (2) That God's word has always condemned division.
    - (a) 1 Corinthians 1:10; John 17:20; Ephesians 4:4, 5.
  - (3) That a church built by men is not "as good as" one built by Christ (Psa. 127:1).
  - (4) That a church that cost efforts of men is not "as good as" one that cost the blood of Christ.
  - (5) That a church that is unknown to the Scriptures is not "as good as" one found in the Bible.
- e. Catholicism did not take all this sitting down but began a bloody persecution against all Protestants.
  - (1) St. Bartholomew's Day Massacre (1574) in France. 70,000 Huguenots (French Protestants) were killed in one day.
  - (2) Many fled to England and eventually to America to escape these persecutions.

5. The Restoration Movement of 1790 to the present time.
   - a. NOTE: Not trying to reform either Catholicism or denominationalism but simply to restore the church as taught in the New Testament.

NOTES

(1) To take the pattern or blue-print given by inspired men and follow it without addition or subtraction.
    (a) Restore any practice or teaching that had been neglected or ignored by men.
    (b) Throw out anything added since the days of the apostles by human authority.
(2) To plant the same seed (gospel) that was planted in the last century, knowing that this seed of the Kingdom (Luke 8:11) would always produce simply Christians.
(3) They preached the same gospel, wore the same name, had the same simple organization, engaged in the same work, and worshiped as the early church – they were in reality, the New Testament church restored.
(4) The plea of the church of Christ today is to come back with us beyond the existence denominationalism with its division and confusion, beyond the existence of Catholicism with its corruptions back to the church as it existed in its purity in the days of he Apostles.
    (a) We do not preach or practice anything that we cannot give a "thus saith the Lord" for.
    (b) We do not require of any person as a condition of salvation that which they cannot read for themselves in the Word of God.

III. The Essentiality of the Church.

A. There is a common misconception in the religious world that the church is a non-essential institution. They attempt to distinguish between "salvation in Christ" and "church membership." But to the careful student of the Bible such a distinction is ridiculous. Christ is "all things in all" to the church – there is no acceptable relationship you can sustain to Christ outside of His church. In saying this we are not teaching "church salvation," as we understand clearly that Jesus is the savior, not the church. However, what we are stressing is that the church is that realm or relationship in which this salvation is enjoyed and realized.

B. This truth can be easily demonstrated by using the different figures used to designate the church.
1. The house of God (1 Tim. 3:15; Eph. 2:19).
    a. Christ is "over" this house (Heb. 3:6), if we are not in the house of God (the church), Christ is not "over" us, He is not our Elder Brother.
    b. Unless we are in this house, or family, we are not heirs of God (Rom. 8:16, 17).
    c. Unless we are in God's house (or family) we do not have the right to "call upon Him as Father" (1 Pet. 1:17-24).
2. The kingdom (Matt. 16:18, 19).
    a. Christ is the "King of kings and Lord of lords" (Rev. 19:16), but if we are not in His Kingdom (the church), He is neither our King nor our Lord.
    b. Those who have been "translated into this Kingdom" are said to be (Col. 1):
        (1) "Saints and faithful brethren in Christ" (v. 2).
        (2) "Partakers of the inheritance of the saints in light" (v. 12).
        (3) Redeemed and forgiven (v. 14).

NOTES

            (4) Reconciled (v. 22).
            (5) Outside of the kingdom (or church) none of these things could be said of them.
        c. When Jesus comes again, there are a certain class of people who will be delivered up to God. Who are they? Those in the kingdom (church) (1 Cor. 15:24).
    3. Church.
        a. Acts 2:47 – If God adds all the saved to the church, then all those outside of the church are unsaved.
        b. Acts 20:28; Ephesians 5:25. Would Jesus have died for a non-essential institution? The value of anything can usually be determined by the price paid for it. If you place any value on the blood of Christ, you should value equally the church that He purchased with His blood.
    4. Body (Eph. 1:22, 23).
        a. Christ is the Head of this body. If we remain out of this body, we deny Jesus the right to rule over us and control our lives.
        b. Christ is the savior, but of whom? Not the whole world (1 Cor. 11:32), but the body (or church) (Eph. 5:23).
        c. Only in the body (church) are we reconciled to God (Eph. 2:13).
    5. Zion (Heb. 12:22-25).
        a. Divine prophecy said that God would place "salvation in Zion" (Isa. 46:13). But Zion is the church, therefore, out of the church we cannot have that salvation.
        b. Those in Zion (the church) have their names "written in Heaven." How important it is for us to be in the church and have our names enrolled in God's Book of Life is seen in Revelation 20:15.
    6. Temple (1 Cor. 3:16).
        a. Christ is the High Priest in this spiritual temple (Heb. 4:14), unless we are in the temple (church) we cannot offer acceptable worship through Him (1 Pet. 2:5).
        b. God dwells by His Spirit in the temple (the church) (Eph. 2:21, 22). If we want to walk with God, live with God, feel God's presence in our lives, we must be in this realm where God dwells.
    7. In Christ.
        a. That the expressions "in Christ" and "in the church" are synonymous is evident from the fact that it takes the same steps to put us into both:
            (1) Faith and baptism put us INTO CHRIST (Gal. 3:26, 27).
            (2) Faith and baptism put us INTO THE CHURCH (Acts 2:21, 47).
            (3) Faith and baptism save us (Mark 16:16).
        b. Since the "fullness" of Christ is found in the church (Eph. 1:23), it is obvious that all of the blessings that are described as being "in Christ," can be enjoyed only in the church.

NOTES

Conclusion:

From the beginning of time God has planned and purposed a spiritual institution for man's development and preparation for an eternal home with Him. Jesus died on the cross to make this church a reality. In spite of the confusion and division that apostasy has created, that one church still exists today. Your salvation, your relationship to Christ, your eternal hope depends upon your being a faithful member of that church.

NOTES

BIBLIOGRAPHY

The Bible (ASV).
Transformist Illusion, Douglas Dewar.
Divine Demonstration, Everest.
In His Image, Wm. Jennings Bryan.
The Truth of Christianity, W. T. Turton.
Internal Evidences of Christianity, Homer Hailey.
The Unrealized Logic of Religion, W. H. Fitchett.
Why We Believe in Creation, not Evolution, Fred Meldau.
Another Look at Evolution, Gordon Wilson.
Paley's Works, Vol. I and 2.
Bulwarks of the Faith, Foy E. Wallace, Jr., Vols. 1 and 2.
Why I Believe in God, Raymond Kelcy.
Basis of Faith, E. R. Conder.
Science is a Sacred Cow, Anthony Standen.
Origin of Species, Darwin.
Descent of Man, Darwin.
Bales-Teller Debate.
Meaning of Evolution, Geo. Gaylord Simpson.
Tract, "Evolution v. the New World."
Pocket Bible Handbook, Halley.
All About the Bible, Sidney Collett.
Why We Believe the Bible, Geo. DeHoff.
Modern Science and the Christian Faith, American Scientific Affiliation.
Reason and Revelation, Milligan.
Evidences of Christianity, Mark Hopkins.
Hastings Bible Dictionary.
Ancient Faith in Conflict (Florida College Lectures).
Organan of Scripture, J. S. Lamar.
General Biblical Introduction, H. S. Miller.
God's Prophetic Word, Foy E. Wallace, Jr.
Thayer's Greek-English Lexicon.
Expositor's Dictionary of New Testament Words, W. E. Vine.
Bishop Newton on the Prophecies.
Prophecies Unveiled, A M. Morris.
Trench on Miracles.
Chief End of Revelation, A. B. Bruce.
Archeology and the Bible, Sir Fredrick Kenyan.
Josephus's *Complete Works*.
Introduction to the Study of the Gospels, Westcott.
The Man of Galilee, A. G. Haygood.
The Life of Christ, Farrar (2 Vol.)
The Life and Times of Jesus, Edersheim (2 Vol.)
Walking by Faith, Roy Cogdili.
Catholicism Against Itself, O. C. Lambert.
Christian System, Campbell.
Notes on Baptist Doctrine, Jim Cope.

www.ingramcontent.com/pod-product-compliance
Lightning Source LLC
Chambersburg PA
CBHW080941040426
42444CB00015B/3401